Sarah Matilda Henry Davis

**Norway Nights and Russian Days**

Vol. 1

Sarah Matilda Henry Davis

**Norway Nights and Russian Days**
*Vol. 1*

ISBN/EAN: 9783337297572

Hergestellt in Europa, USA, Kanada, Australien, Japan

Cover: Foto ©Thomas Meinert / pixelio.de

Weitere Bücher finden Sie auf **www.hansebooks.com**

# *Norway Nights*
## *&* *Russian Days.*

BY

## S. M. HENRY DAVIS,

AUTHOR OF "LIFE AND TIMES OF SIR PHILIP SIDNEY."

𝔚𝔦𝔱𝔥 Numerous Illustrations.

*Norwegian Peasant.*

NEW YORK:

FORDS, HOWARD, & HULBERT.

1887.

To

# Mꭹ Son

*I INSCRIBE THIS RECORD OF A
PLEASANT SUMMER TOUR.*

# CONTENTS.

# ILLUSTRATIONS.

## NORWAY NIGHTS.

## RUSSIAN DAYS.

# NORWAY NIGHTS.

# NORWAY NIGHTS.

## CHAPTER I.

### SETTING OUT.

" Thor had two ravens, Hugin and Mugin, who flew all over the world and brought him news from every quarter."

IN defiance of the conservative old adage, a party of three rolling stones started out to gather moss in Norway and its adjacent countries. Moreover, they did gather it : rich, vivid, aromatic, health-giving to mind and body, joy in acquisition, a treasure in memory.

The progress of the travellers developed harmony of purpose, of disposition, and of taste ; and the tour was also singularly favored by the ele-

ments and by circumstances: no cold, no heat;
timely showers, but not one day of rain ; no failure
to meet trains or steamers ; the best rooms in the
best hotels ; obliging landlords and civil attendants
everywhere. They had wisely started early in the
season, before managers became excited and servants overworked by the pressure of tourists,
while rooms were fresh and visitors fair to behold.
But yet more of their comfort was due to the
good and kindly nature of the Scandinavians
whose territory they invaded. Anglo-Saxons of
to-day are paying back the incursions of the old
Norse pirates a thousand years ago, but with better feeling on both sides.

This pleasant journey of three women—neither
"lone" nor "lorn"—began the first day of June,
1886. There is a choice in the liquid paths to
Norway. One is from Hull or Newcastle in
England by the North Sea to Bergen : another, in
smoother waters, from Danish Copenhagen to

Christiania; and a third line of steamers, swift
and well appointed, has lately been built to sail
from Aberdeen to the western coast of Norway,
taking in the principal places there, and also running away up to the North Cape.

It pleased us better, with perhaps an instinct of
the kind embodied in the proverb—*Reculer pour
mieux sauter*—to first turn southward. Thus,
after receiving a benediction in Cologne Cathedral,
we glided slowly up the river which is so vain of
its castles and clamorous of its legends, to gay,
complacent Frankfort : thence, turning northward
again, we paused at Cassel, which redeems its
commonplace streets by its Auegarten, one of the
most beautiful public parks in Germany, dignified
by superb oaks and a winding river,—and which
also boasts of an admirable picture-gallery, and of
the castle and park of Wilhelmshöhe where Napoleon III. was a reluctant "guest" after his fatal
defeat at Sedan. Another day we gave to pros-

perous, pretty Hanover, and two or three to Hamburg, where we enjoyed its gay gardens, its charming Alster promenade, and its general air of success. It was on the *menu* of the Hamburger Hof that we were offered a sort of fritter with the unmeaning name of "Armer Ritter," and an article called "Lieder ohne Worte," which of course ought to have been a dish of skylarks, but was merely beefsteak with a mysterious sauce. Next in order on our chart was the railway, still northward, across the much-*bequestioned* Schleswig-Holstein to the little town of Kiel, which although not large is important, being the home-station of the principal part of the German navy, that finds both refuge and anchorage in its deep fiord. From Kiel one goes by steam around the eastern islands of Denmark nine or ten hours to Copenhagen.

The shores of the fiord are pleasing, but not salient ; many islands dot the waters, and the villages resemble toy hamlets with bright yellow houses and red roofs. The steamer was severely clean, and gratuitously furnished minute guidebooks in various languages, those in English being peculiarly eulogistic of "the view of the aspect of the sceneries."

Here we first heard the language of Denmark and Norway, rather blunt and unmusical, and with so slight analogy to any other that memory retains it with difficulty. A few nouns and phrases for travelling purposes are of course desirable, and well worth the trouble of acquiring. In fact, it is better to take a good deal of trouble rather than endure the humiliating sense of helpless idiocy in a foreign land. One is unconsciously apt to fancy that with the accents of a new language one must receive new ideas, as if the problems of thought might clear themselves through strange articulations—a delusion quickly dispelled when we find that such mystic syllables as "Ver saa god luk op dören og luk vinduet

igjen" convey no deeper meaning than "Please
shut the door and open the window."

Copenhagen, as seen on the surface, did not
appeal forcibly to our interest. The streets are
broad, modern, and indistinctive. There are
pretty drives—one especially around the harbor,
where hundreds of masts with foreign and native
flags are etched against the evening sky—and an indented coast studded with trees, well "composed"
as a picture. On a wooded hill above is a substantial, comfortable-looking Mariner's Home, a
pleasing contrast to the wretched boarding-houses
and drinking-caves, where those homeless sea-birds
often find their only refuge. The old castle of
Rosenberg standing in a fine park is curious as
the residence of a long line of Danish kings,
whose ugly portraits decorate the stuffy interior.
One could readily believe that the handsome windows in old German style had never admitted
fresh air since the last breath of the last of the

"Christians" had feebly floated through them.
The good-looking Hercules who conducted us
through the rooms told us, in excellent and hu-
morous English, several anecdotes of these de-
funct royalties, and exhibited, with an interest that
became contagious, their quaintly-embroidered
satin coats and dresses, old jewel- and snuff-boxes,
watches, gold goblets, silver andirons, and much
more of that indescribable lumber which becomes
either art-treasure or rubbish according to the
taste of succeeding ages. Our cicerone's air of
*bonhomie* and pleasant jests indicated a social
grade quite above that of an ordinary guide; and
the perplexing question whether or not to offer
him the customary fee nearly proved our disgrace.
Fortunately he relieved our unexpressed dilemma
by indicating that the servant whom he had ordered to bring us a branch of lilac-blossoms
would not object to a gratuity. We afterwards
learned that he was by no means the ordinary

showman, but the "Herr Direktor" of the palace, and inferred that it was probably for the mere pleasure of talking that he had played the part of Boswell to his dead lions.

The principal object of interest in Copenhagen is Thorwaldsen's gallery, which occupies three stories in a large building erected for that purpose, and contains the original casts of nearly all his works. Although his sculptures are familiar objects all over Europe, and plaster copies are universal, only here does one realize the creative power and manual industry of the genial sculptor. The most interesting of his later productions is an unfinished life-size statue of himself leaning on a youthful figure of Hope. In this as in all portraits of him there is an almost childlike sweetness of expression, as well as vivacious intelligence in his strongly-marked features. There are several lions in plaster and marble, but they give only a faint impression of the magnificent creature carved in the face of the rock at Lucerne, where, overshadowed by lofty trees, his gigantic body reflected in the water, but unapproachable to the profane touch of the curious, he lies dying, alone, in pathetic majesty.

This temple of art is built around a court in the centre of which is the artist's grave ; utterly simple, in accordance with his directions : only an ivy-covered mound enclosed by low slabs of granite, with the name "Thorwaldsen" carved on one side, on another the dates of his birth and death—that single word his all-sufficient eulogy.

When leaving Copenhagen we quite forgot that the sail to Elsinore would lead us to the alleged locality of Hamlet's grave, marked by a heap of stones ; but as that young hero's life is by latest researches supposed to antedate the Christian Era by two hundred years, one may be pardoned for not sacrificing on so mythical a shrine.

We embarked for Christiania on the fine Danish steamer *Melchior ;* but as it came from Stettin with full complement of passengers, we were unable to obtain private sleeping-cabins, and it became a serious question whether we should not be obliged to sit up all night.   Happily, the captain's kindness, added to a slight knowledge of English and German, came to the rescue, and he ordered the large deck-saloon to be placed at our disposal after 10 P.M.   This was the first of a series of gratuitous courtesies which we received from the chief officers of ten different steamers in northern waters ; for which we hold them in grateful remembrance.

Here was our first noticeable experience of a June sunrise in higher latitudes.   Wakened at half-past two by the light glowing through uncurtained windows, I stepped on deck to breathe the first freshness of that perfect day.   The sky was scintillant with opaline hues ; the water, a tremulous mass of jewels in the wake of the golden sun : and the beauty was even heightened by solitude, for not a creature was visible, save one red-capped sailor at the prow.

# CHAPTER II.

THE voyage to Christiania is made in about twenty hours, and during at least half that time the ship steers between verdant islands of various forms and sizes. The fiord that leads directly from the Baltic to Christiania is fifty miles long, including the Kattegat and Skagger Rack of childish amusement in foreign names, narrowing and widening between Denmark and Sweden, —a very picturesque arm of the sea, enlivened by sailing-boats and steamers, flecked with islands, and bounded by fertile, sometimes pine-clad, hills dotted with pleasant-looking villas.

The new capital of Norway is unmarked by steeples or any salient architectural lines. As we neared the harbor, a little fleet of twenty sailing-vessels glided towards us, simulating, in the morning mist that now partially obscured the sun, a procession of white robed and hooded Carmelite monks, in twos and threes, the smaller ones behind in pictural perspective, going out to morning prayer. The beauty of that June morning, and of the lovely panorama, might well inspire a *Te Deum laudamus.*

Here we were at last, in the Norway of our dreams—very different dreams from those of the Orient, of Italy and Spain : a land of the grandly picturesque, dark and stern in most of its moods as were the anthropomorphic gods of its pagan days, and with a simple, honest, practical people who are the antipodes of Southern fire and Eastern guile.

As the landing-plank was secured to the quay, a few porters and cabmen stood quietly waiting, some of whom came on board with grave salutations, and carried off on their stalwart shoulders the boxes of a hundred or more equally tranquil passengers. No one shrieked or pushed or lost temper, and yet the end was accomplished without these ordinary motors. The customhouse officers, with national trust in the probity of their fellow-beings, merely asked for a declaration, without opening a trunk.

We soon found ourselves in such attractive rooms at the Victoria Hotel that we said in our hearts, ''Let us abide here forever.'' It was not a ''grand hotel,''—happily we were not doomed in Norway to those mocking hostelries that are fain to pass themselves off as palaces, and to give you the minimum of comfort with the maximum of price,—but a serene *quasi*-home, where one receives the respectful tribute of his own name, and is not stigmatized as Number Twenty-nine. In our ''ideal tour,'' as we fondly called it, we escaped that obloquy everywhere. We breakfasted here in a veranda open on one side to a garden,

and profusely decorated on the others with polar-
bear skins, eider - down rugs, reindeer and elk
heads and antlers, a collection of antique silver
ornaments, carved-wood trifles, eider-ducks and
auks that looked alive but for their immobility,
besides enticing photographs of waterfalls and
mountains. The prettiest-mannered little thing in
feathers hopped on the back of a chair close by
our table, cocked his head on one side inquiringly,
but without even the chirp of a petition : evidently a reconnoitring party sent out to scan the
resources and disposition of the enemy ; for when
an amicable volley of crumbs was projected towards him he flew away, but presently returned
with half a dozen of his tiny brothers.

The dining-room was a pretty pavilion in the
garden, covered with striped red and white linen :
from the roof were suspended with friendly inter-
national effect the flags of various countries : a
huge mass of sparkling ice rose like a glacier from

the centre of the table, around which gathered
Danes, Swedes, Germans, one or two Frenchmen
(who always look out of place when out of
France), and Englishmen garrulous of prospective
spoils in trout and reindeer haunts. Some years
ago Norway was an El Dorado of freedom for
sportsmen, but several Englishmen have purchased
or leased large estates of the best salmon-grounds
(or waters), and the government now exacts a tax
on public lands of two hundred to three hundred
krone (or ten to fifteen pounds sterling) for the
season. Salmon-fishing is not now to be obtained ; but other fishing is always at hand, and
reindeer may be hunted if one will take a guide to
their mountain haunts and accept the hardships
involved in the pursuit of creatures so shy and
keen-scented. Sleeping on straw in a leaky hut
or under a snow-covered rock, with only milk and
oat-cakes to live upon, certainly demands the
noble incentive of "something to kill."

Christiania, which replaced a much older town, was founded in 1624 by Christian IV. of Denmark. It is built mostly of stone, the original city of wood having suffered from many conflagrations; the streets are broad to avoid this danger, and the houses low, generally only two stories. It cannot be called architecturally handsome, but has a few fine streets, the best of which contains the principal shops and has a lively aspect. At one end is the Storthing, or Parliament House, a more curious than happy combination of Romanesque and Renaissance styles outside, but very comfortable within. The other terminus is a pretty park which leads to a hill of moderate height, on which stands the very plain but substantial royal palace. In front of this edifice is a statue of Bernadotte, first king of Sweden and Norway, on a pedestal carved with the words,

" The people's love is my reward."

—a sentiment which during at least the early part of his reign was rather more theoretical than practical; for Norway, wrested from Denmark after a union of four hundred years by the *haute politique* of Russia and Sweden combined, was much more disposed to receive the *parvenu* monarch with cuffs than with kisses, and with pardonable patriotism resisted all attempts to infringe upon its free Constitution. However, not to plunge unduly into history, Bernadotte, successful adventurer, soldier, and statesman as he was, had wisdom enough to make many popular concessions, and his successors have proved acceptable rulers. But it is evident even to a passing traveller that the old jealousies are not quite effaced between the united kingdoms. Norway clings proudly and fondly to the traditions and institutions of "Gammle Norge"—old Norway—and observes with considerable pride the anniversary of May 17, 1814, when the mutual rights of king and people were clearly defined and guaranteed by the allied powers. The government is more republican than monarchical ; there is no hereditary nobility ; the two houses of Parliament combine much freedom with judicious checks upon each other ; a bill which has passed through both houses of three successive assemblies of parliament may become a law without the royal assent ; and there are reasonable property qualifications for the privilege of voting.

The interior of the palace is utterly unpalatial, the only objects worth looking at being a few pictures by the most celebrated native artists, Tiderman and Gude. The Queen's apartments are very unpretending, but have a happy air from the numerous photographs and portraits that cover walls and tables. We noticed a picture of a sheaf of oats hanging from a window in wintertime, and were told that it illustrated the pretty custom of giving Christmas dinner to the birds.

The broad balcony of the palace commands a charming view of the city, the neighboring hills dotted with villas, the bay flecked with white sails, and the graceful curves of the shore. The castle of Agershaus, six hundred years old, stands prominently on one of the hills, a fortress and also a prison. A story is told of an adroit criminal, the Robin Hood of Norway, who was long ago imprisoned here in a room formed of thick iron bars. After having several times eluded the jailers (once by breaking into the inspector's room while that official was at church, dressing in his clothes and quietly walking out of the city), he was consigned to a deep dungeon underneath the strongest part of the fortress, whence escape seemed impossible. But like Love he laughed at bolts and bars, cut through the heavy planks of the flooring, and made an outlet under the walls. Not long after he robbed a bank of a large amount. so mysteriously as to leave no trace on either door or locks;

and finally, on being again imprisoned, gave the last turn to his fate by hanging himself.

A well-shaded drive up the hills brought us to the little summer palace called Oscar's Hall, which seems to have no *raison d'être* except the view, the rooms being small and nearly bare. On the dining-room walls hang a set of paintings by Tiderman, depicting with great charm of color and form Norwegian peasant-life from infancy to old age. The favorite subjects of this popular artist were taken from his own people, and probably no one has given the world so faithful an idea of their characteristics. On his crowded canvas is no indistinctness or confusion; the grouping is artistic, and the varied and marked expressions of face an admirable study.

A few steps from Oscar's Hall there stands on a grassy slope a very small wooden chapel, which is a most fantastic piece of architecture, and closely resembles a very ancient one at Borgund, and an-

ANCIENT CHURCH.

other at Hitterdal near Bergen. The interior, which will not hold more than fifty people, has no windows, and light is admitted only from the two doors; a covered balcony runs all around the building, and a lofty indescribable roof surmounts it, ornamented with serpents twined together, and dragons' heads, more Chinese than European. In the other churches of the same sort are relics of pagan forms of worship.

Nearly opposite this "Gammle Kirke" is a quaint old peasant-house containing furniture, kitchen utensils, beds, and the family Bible precisely as they were left two hundred years ago; and at that time the low-raftered ceiling, tiny windows, and painfully short beds in close alcoves or bunks were perhaps considered a "grateful shelter."

There is a flourishing small university in Christiania, and an interesting museum, with a picture-gallery containing some good paintings by native artists, all of whom, however, study in Düsseldorf or Paris, as there is no school of art in Norway. The ethnographical department illustrates the

household life of two centuries ago in carved furniture, quaint utensils, silver ornaments, spoons
and cups. There is great skill exhibited in this
work, especially in the filigree : in all the towns,

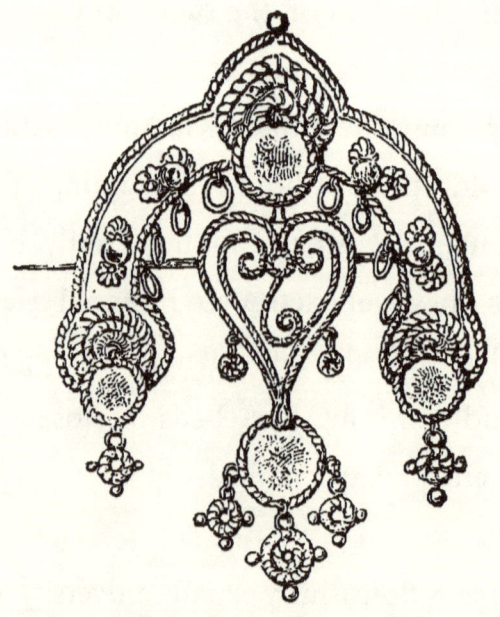

OLD NORWEGIAN BROOCH.

and even in the villages, silversmiths are numerous.
The antique spoons are awkward in shape, but
the handles are often curiously wrought. In those
made by the Laplanders, found farther north,

small, finely-chased rings are inserted; silver brooches and wedding-rings were similarly adorned, as well as by rows of gilded ornaments, like the bowl of a salt-spoon. Modern collectors have swept away the greater part of these interesting relics; in a short time there will be scarcely an old spoon left outside of museums. Hitherto the peasants emigrating to America have often sold their silver heirlooms; but they never part with them if they can help it. Among these *curios* is one group that brings a shudder—the girdle and knives used in the duel which prevailed among the lower classes until about sixty years ago. The combatants began by driving their knives into a piece of wood; that portion of each blade not buried in the wood was bound around with strips of leather, leaving for use only the part which the wielder had been able to stab into the wood. The men were now placed close together face to face, the girdle around both,

securely buckled so that neither could release himself; their knives were handed them, and they
fought till one of them gave out. This coarse
and horrible mode of settling a grievance was
known as "the duel of the girdle." It is said that
as these duels were almost certain to be fatal to
one or both parties, every man's wife used to
carry a winding-sheet to banquets where quarrels
were likely to arise from jealousy or intoxica-
tion.

In the picturesque market-place stands the oldest church, the interest of which is all on the outside, looking down upon the vendors of domestic
wares, scanty vegetables and fruits, the best of
which at this season are the fragrant little · wild
strawberries.

Two or three days are quite sufficient for a good
view of Christiania, including the near excursions,
for its area contains only one hundred and fifty
thousand inhabitants. A local guide - book,

"printed at expenses of the author," contains
some amusing specimens of English learned in
Norway. He says, "In Oslo is the very old Oslo
church situated. It is built in a very old style and
is very old." He mentions "several establishments
for informations, destinated for boys and girls,
together with many others establishments founded
for more specially use." He proudly enumerates
the "not quite inconsiderable" manufactories of
Christiania, among which is a "fabric for pack
of cards;" and says, "the streets are altogether
well-pavemented and in the night lightened with
gas." The Hotel Victoria "is undergone several
new amendments after the present pretensions,"
and "is put to the stranger's disposition for it
exists no public restauration there." The stranger
is advised to "accord with the coachman so as
to escape later incommodations," and invited to a
"great plain which is used for exercising the soldiers of every arms ; these march off from the city

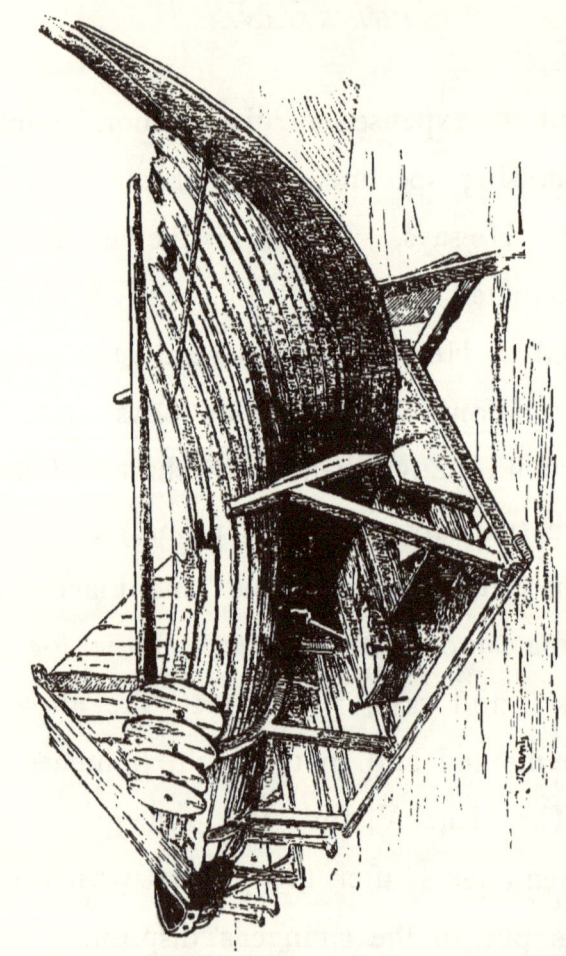

REMAINS OF VIKING SHIP—SHOWING SHIELDS.

in the morning and return in the evening ; no more notice of this " !  The table of contents includes "a trip to the Madhouse," "a trip to the deafs and dumbs," "the fire-stopping apparates," and other equally well-defined sights.

The most interesting object to be seen in the city of Christiania is the celebrated Viking ship which was found buried at Gokstad, a little town on the southern coast in a tumulus called the King's Mound, from the tradition that a king had been buried there with his valuables.

But, as all the world now knows, the Vikings and the Sea-Kings were two distinct classes of Norse folk ; the latter being really of royal race, while the former were roving pirates who found refuge for their long rowing-galleys in the *vicks*, or creeks, of the coast.  Probably in modern American parlance we should call them *Creekers ;* still, *Viking* has a royal and romantic sound, and we will not give it up.  Doubtless they were formidable in their time, whatever we may now call them.

In 1880 the owners of the land excavated the vessel with its numerous appurtenances, archæologists hastened to see and speculate, fragments were carefully criticised, and finally the entire treasure-trove was transferred to Christiania, where a wooden building was erected for it. It is the largest and most complete ship in the world of so ancient date,—A.D. 900,—and had evidently been the private property of one of those Viking pirates who bore terror at his prow and conquest at his helm.

> "The eagle heads of all the North
>     Have left their stormy strand ;
> The warriors of the world set forth
>     To seek another land.
> Again their long keels sheer the wave,
>     Their broad sails court the breeze ;
> Again the reckless and the brave
>     Ride, lords of weltering seas."

This curious craft was seventy-six feet long, sixteen feet wide amidships, had a lofty prow, a single mast with a square sail, and was clinker-built— that is, the lower edge of every plank overlaps the next below it like slates on the roof of a house. It contained the remains of three small boats even more remarkable than the vessel itself, as the only known specimen of so great antiquity. They are of unpainted oak, very sharp at each end, with a place for a mast, singular rowlocks for oars, and are most skilfully wrought, even the bottom-boards being adorned with graven circles. The ship was originally equipped with thirty-two shields, but only four now remain. Their disks were formed of thin white pine and a central boss, a cross-piece underneath serving as handle. Each shield was so arranged that its outer edge touched the boss of the preceding one ; and as they were painted yellow and black, the whole range looked like a series of party-colored half-moons. They were probably.

REMAINS OF VIKING SHIP—STARBOARD SIDE, SHOWING RUDDER.

from their thinness, indifferent defences, for the Sagas often speak of shields being cleft and exchanged for new ones. Possibly they were designed more for ornament than for use.

A very interesting object is the rudder, which is in perfect preservation on the starboard—originally the *steerboard*, or steering—side, which here is on the right of the vessel. It was evidently a sort of movable blade or oar, not attached to the ship, but to a projecting beam of wood, and could be hauled on deck when the oars were used instead of sails. The one mast was also movable, and when erected was placed in a hole made in a beam at the bottom of the ship, and secured a few feet higher up by passing through another orifice in a heavy log of curious shape. There were no indications of seats for the rowers, who may have plied the oars in a standing position, in manner similar to that of Venetian gondoliers.

Among the relics found with the ship are the

feathers of a peacock, no doubt a souvenir of foreign voyages ; a bundle of yellow cloth with red
stripes sewed on, clearly meant for a tent ; dark-
gray woollen fragments of clothing, a long piece
of silk interwoven with gold, carved wooden
plates, cups, candlesticks, gilded and silvered
strap-buckles and buttons, a large copper caldron, a remarkable axe, and even the landing-
plank. Who knows but this plank may have upheld the feet of the adventurous Norsemen who
sought new homes among the geysers of Iceland
before pushing over to America, or who crushed
heather and gorse in Scotland, or even of those
who stepped from the Golden Horn to service in
the Imperial Guard of the Sultan's palace ! *

The funeral of a Viking chief was a barbaric

---

* I give considerable space to the description of this
old ship, because it was really the most characteristic
and historically interesting thing to be seen in Norway.

ceremony. A slight excavation was made on the coast, into which his ship was lowered, the prow turned seaward. A sepulchral cabin was prepared in the centre, and the body, lying on a sledge, decked in state attire, ornaments and full panoply of arms, was then introduced, and the opening closed with layers of birch-bark ; all other personal possessions were laid in other parts of this gigantic coffin, which was packed to the top with moss and blue clay, which is said to be a peculiarly good preservative against decay. His horses and dogs were killed and placed against the sides, and finally earth piled over all in form of a lofty mound. This was done very near the shore, so that even after death the shadow of the sea-rover might frown upon his chosen element. Occasionally, however, the vessel and its owner were burned together to the water's edge. A tradition has come down concerning one of those dauntless warriors that when he felt the hand of death upon him he ordered his ship to be filled with combustible materials and ignited, the sail set seaward, and there, alone upon his funeral-pyre, the spray of ocean for his chrism, the winds his ministers, his unconquered spirit fled to the Walhalla of his faith.

Even ships "may rise on stepping-stones of former selves." Perhaps a thousand years hence the skeleton of one of our ocean steamers may survive—a barbaric toy, when the now-anticipated glories of electric motors shall have had their day, and some more powerful agent may offer summer excursions straight to the Pole itself.

# CHAPTER III.

BEFORE leaving Christiania we planned our chart of travel with the aid of Mr. Bennett, an Englishman long resident there, who is a sort of Cook's Agency amplified and improved. He rents vehicles for posting, marks out routes in accordance with the time and taste of the inquirer, furnishes guide-books, has a large assortment of antiquities for sale, and is withal so friendly and obliging that he is very popular. Our time was limited, for we had also Sweden and Russia before us, and an engagement at Bayreuth at the end of two months.

It has been well said that two of the requisites for a pleasant tour are "a little too little time and a little too much money." The spur of action stimulates the brain ; the generous purse secures from care. The *quantum sufficit* in Scandinavia is somewhat less than elsewhere on the Continent, and is indicated in a general way in the guide-books. Mr. Bennett is especially serviceable to ladies travelling without a courier, and they can very well dispense with one on ordinary routes if they will take the trouble to learn a little Norsk. A few lessons only are necessary for pronunciation, and Bennett's Phrase-book is more helpful than those books generally are, being more ingeniously arranged. If a guide is preferred, a man in Christiania named Aak may be highly recommended.

Our route was to take us up the Mjösen lake, the largest in Norway, to Lilliehamar, thence across the Gudbransdal and the Romsdal valleys to Molde, including the Geiranger Fiord, to the western coast ; from Molde to Trondhjem ; thence by steamer to the North Cape. Much patient scrutiny of numerous guide-books had indicated this as a very satisfactory though not an exhaustive tour. For the latter at least one entire, diligent summer would be required, and even then much would be left out.

A railway ride of two hours through a fertile country for that latitude brought us to Eidsvold, where we went on board the *Kong Oscar*, a dainty little steamer affording an upper deck and a good dinner, including the inevitable Lax or salmon. The simple-hearted old captain paid us frequent visits and expatiated on the beauties of the lake, which he had thoroughly learned in his experience of thirty years between its two principal points. It is the largest in Norway, seventy miles long, and contains twenty species of fish, whose ancestors must have suffered terrible fright during the earthquake at Lisbon in 1755, when the waves suddenly rose twenty feet high and as suddenly retreated. The banks are pleasing, but have no salient features, until at the northern end the hills rise in height with evident emulation of their neighbors in the Gudbransdal region ; forests of birch and mountain ash grow to the water's edge, and pine and fir reach to their summits. All day we saw drifting down to Eidsvold rafts of pine logs felled in mountain forests, where they are shot singly down the Lougen (a tributary of the lake), over boulders and cataracts, as far as Lilliehamar ; there they are collected and bound together for a new itinerary.

We stopped for the night at Lilliehamar, a prosperous but not a pretty village in spite of its pretty name (Little Hill) and its commanding position above Lake Mjösen. Like nearly all Norwegian villages it consists mainly of one long straggling street of uninviting houses, in which are half a dozen shops that offer in the murky windows hats, buttons, colored handkerchiefs, faded photographs,

and pebbly bonbons. However, it considers itself a promising town and boasts of several mills,
a "grammar school," and two or three rival inns.
We went to the ambitiously-named Victoria, which
overlooks the lake. Its bare floors and deficiency
of toilet requisites suggested "roughing it," but
through our emphatic gestures and our few invalu-
able Norse words the bewildered landlady con-
trived to understand enough of our needs to
make us comfortable. After our excellent supper of brook trout and wheat pancakes, or
"pankagen," which are a specialty of Norway,
the captain of the *Kong Oscar* walked up from
his boat to escort us to a neighboring waterfall
which for the honor of his country he was fain to
exhibit. A pleasant saunter through fragrant
woods and wild-flowers led to a point where the
turbulent little river Messna dashes and dances
over a heap of boulders in a very spirited manner.
"Helvedeshöl," or "Caldron of Hell," seemed a

needlessly severe name for a rush of water that was merely in high (not evil) spirits.

We declined an invitation to watch departing day with other guests on the terrace at eleven o'clock, and began to wonder whether anybody ever went to bed o' summer nights in Norway. Our first sweet sleep had scarcely begun when cocks and hens announced the sun again, and reminded us that we had appointed an early hour for our first experiment in the national vehicles, cariole, stolkjærre, and trille. The kariol, or cariole, of Norway, unlike our carryall which its name suggests, is a unique vehicle—a species of gig with two wheels, for one person only. It is light and simple in construction ; the long, elastic shafts are attached to the axle-tree ; the seat, placed well forward, rests by cross-pieces upon the shafts. The legs of the rider must be nearly horizontal and rest on stirrup-shaped irons, so that he is protected from all inconvenience and danger in descending

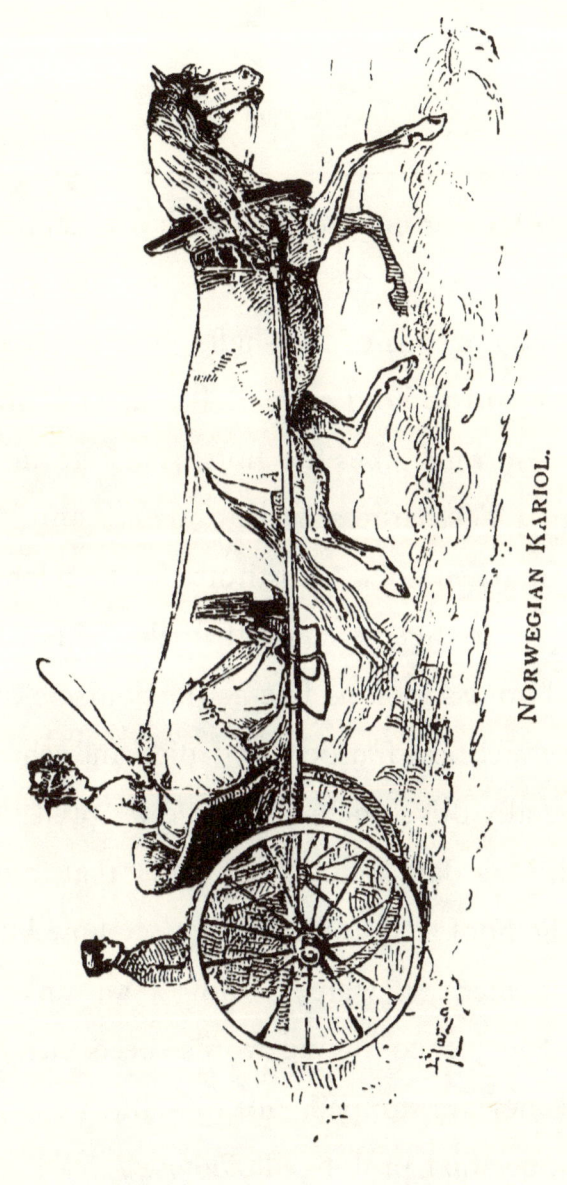

NORWEGIAN KARIOL.

steep hills or in case of the horse falling—a rare
occurrence, as the animals are very sure-footed.
Across the ends of the shafts, behind the seat, there
is a board to hold a small trunk, and on that sits
the boy who takes the horse back to his post-station. The harness has no traces, and the shafts
are attached to a substitute for a collar by some
simple arrangement, so that the little cream-col-
ored ponies look as free as the coursers of Apollo,
but much less frantic, for ladies and children can
generally drive them with safety ; pretty creatures
with long dark manes, and tails that often reach
to the hoof. It is pleasant to see how kindly they
are treated : a whip is almost an unknown appendage ; encouraging words speed them forward,
and they are stopped, not by pulling the reins, but
by a peculiar prolonged *Bur-r-r !*

Like everything else in Norway they move at
rather moderate pace, except down hill, when they
fly like a bicycle and gain impetus for the ascent

beyond. It is a significant fact that only foreigners ever abuse them by hard driving, but it appears
that our high civilization must "get through" at
any cost. Why even *That* should desire to hurry
through picturesque Norway is past comprehen-
sion. It is hard upon the poor farmers, who are
obliged by the government to furnish horses to
travellers in lieu of certain taxes and at fixed and
rather low prices, and particularly disadvantageous
on some of the by-roads, or "slow stations" as
they are called, when in the harvest season the
horses are urgently needed in the fields. Along
the principal arteries of travel the farmers club
together and establish regular "fast," or fixed,
stations, where they always keep in reserve a sufficient number.

Another vehicle, for two or three persons with
a driver, is the *trille*, which cannot be praised
for its "ample space and verge enough," but
otherwise is comfortable—especially if one is for-

tunate, as we were, to obtain a good one for our journey through the Gudbransdal.

We started upon our novel journey from Lilliehamar early in the morning,—early by the clock, very late by the sun,—and a delightfully exciting departure it was. The landlord and land-lady, maids, hostlers, and post-boys assisted with the grave deliberation of the nation, and corded on our portmanteaus, bags, and bundles, previously subjected in Christiania to as stringent limitation as comfort would permit, and we were launched, a fearless, happy trio, upon our own resources and our diamond edition of Norse words, which en-larged itself a little day by day. The cariole was pronounced delightful ; the two in the trille found it satisfactory : and, to vary our experience, we sometimes exchanged places in the two vehicles.

We entered at once the narrow valley of the Gudbransdal, which extends one hundred and fifty miles ; and as far as Dombaas, at the end of

our second day, the valley is rather level. The
mountains on either side are nearly uniform, the
lower slopes cultivated, the heights covered with
pine forests. The Lougen or Laugen, which
merely signifies The River, runs through the valley; sometimes it pauses in smooth swirls which
broaden to a lake, but oftener it forces its milky-
blue waters into narrow channels and foams im-
petuously over stones and boulders, gathers tribute from countless waterfalls in trickling sprays or
dashing torrents, and sweeps down its generous
flood hundreds of huge trees felled from the forests.

At Fossegarden, seven miles from Lilliehamar, is
the cataract called Hunerfos (*fos* means *waterfall*)
that arrests the swim of the abundant lake trout,
which consequently are here caught in large numbers. We sometimes pass huge cairns of stones
which indicate the farmers' trouble in preparing
their land; we obtain on some eminence an oc-

casional glimpse of the snow-capped Rondàne Mountains, seven thousand feet high and tenanted by reindeer and foxes ; and all the way we see patches of snow lingering in crevices, for the 12th of June and the verdure around appeal to them in vain : many of them will hide in the peaks and under ledges of rock all through the summer.

The air is sweet and gracious ; the fields are decked with pink roses, violets, aconite, yellow buttercups, and other spontaneous flowers. The flora of Norway is said to be very abundant for so northern a latitude. Sometimes a linnet in a bush confesses the joy of his heart, and

> "Sings each song thrice over,
>     Lest you should think
>     He never can recapture
>     The first, fine, careless rapture."

Hares flit along the brushwood, harassed by no-body ; pied crows, perched on barns or fences, speculate on our movements ; and now and then a magpie with audacious eye, a bird superstitiously venerated in Norway, tries to intercept our news. Peasants with red woollen caps, tassel hanging from the peak, and odd paniers on their backs, salute us with "Godmorgen." Sunburned children, tidily dressed, lift their clear blue eyes, but never ask for alms. Triangular wooden snowploughs now and then are drawn up from the wayside, suggestive of past and future winter, which in all this summer sheen seems an unseasonable impossibility.

Throughout our six days of posting we had nothing to say but praise—of men, women, and accommodations ; for this is one of the very best posting routes in the country. It is easy enough to find discomforts if one wanders away from the well-beaten tracks. The stations, which are all farm-houses and bear the names of their owners, are from seven to ten miles apart. As we drive

into the enclosure we address the first person we
see with "*Godmorgen ; vær saa god, Heste*"
("Good-morning ; if you please, horses"). No
one properly appreciative of Norwegian civility
would think of omitting "*Vær saa god.*" Travellers who call out peremptorily, "*Heste, strap!*"
("Horses, quick!") are in disfavor among these
quietly courteous people, who from the highest
to the lowest never enter a shop or meet each
other without raising their hats ; who invariably
thank a host or hostess after a repast in the
words "*Tak for Maden*" ("Thanks for the
food"), and receive in reply a hearty "*Velbekom-
men*" ("May it do you good"), and who even
express retrospective gratitude by the frequent
phrase "*Tak for sidst*" ("Thanks for the last time
we met")! When a vehicle overtakes another
on a country road, the driver who desires to pass
the other invariably asks permission, and apolo-
gizes for so doing.

While the farmer or his boys are changing
horses at the stations and a new *Skyds-gut,* or post-
boy, takes his place on each vehicle, we enter the
sitting-room, a pleasant-mannered woman shows us
the *Dag-bog,* or visitors' day-book, where we inscribe
our names in obedience to required custom, also
stating our destination and the number of horses
we require. If there are just causes for complaint,
travellers are requested to enter them ; but these
are very rare, and tributes to the comforts afforded
are numerous. In fact, the farmers themselves are
much more likely to be displeased with the hard
driving of their horses, and are permitted by act
of Parliament, if the animals are injured, to de-
mand an indemnity, on testimony of the post-boy,
two other men being called in to confirm the
claim of injury.

Throughout this valley, which is the most comfortable part of Norway for posting, the farm-
houses are perfectly clean, the sitting-rooms cheer-

ful with pots of growing flowers; heirlooms of
carved or painted furniture are often seen ; views
of the country and numerous family photographs
deck the walls—the latter, it must be said, sometimes ludicrously solemn.    It is not a handsome
race, this honest, kindly race of Norway, and

the sun-artist has not learned
how to idealize by "touching
up" their long, serious faces
and irregular features.    Always we find a few books on
shelves : like the Icelanders,
the people are great readers

NORWEGIAN PEASANT. through the protracted win-
ters.    Education is compulsory, and English is
taught in the higher schools.    The only university
is in Christiania, and the higher classes often send
their boys to England to be educated, and the
girls to Paris or Germany for accomplishments.

We found the beds comfortable as to linen and

eider-down pillows and *duvets* for cool nights ;
but they are decidedly Procrustean for long-limbed
sleepers.

The food, served on coarse white table-linen wo-
ven by hand-looms in the family, is wholesome and
palatable. Beef and mutton are scarcely known ;
but fish, generally trout fresh from the river, veal,
chickens, game, ptarmigan and wood-grouse, dried
reindeer-tongues, — delicate and savory, — good
coffee, milk, eggs, and certain excellent sweets
form a *menu* that ought to satisfy any modern
Lucullus. Of course one never finds them all at a
single repast, fish and one kind of meat or bird
being the rule. The bread is of several sorts—the
coarse family rye bread, white bread for effeminate
foreigners, often imported English biscuits, and invariably the national *Fladbrod*, a round, very thin
and crisp cake about the size of a large dinner-
plate, stamped with tracery, and generally made
of oat or rye meal. Great quantities are prepared

at a time and stowed away in drawers and chests.
Their tea is not the beverage that cheers, and those
who cannot be happy without tea would better take
their own supply.   Pancakes form the usual sweet
dish, and are so delicate that we soon learned to
ask for them at every substantial meal.   They are
generally accompanied by stewed currants or raspberries and whipped cream.   The butter is taste-
less and untempting, and there are no vegetables
except potatoes and a species of sorrel.   Necessarily the quality of the cooking varies : we came
across stations where the *cordon bleu* was decidedly
a *cordon vert.*   The prices are very low : never
more than forty cents, American currency, for dinner or supper ; twenty cents for morning coffee,
eggs, and bread.   We were usually served by the
farmer's wife or daughter, who would speed us at
parting with a kindly " *Farvel ;*" or sometimes by
a *Pige,* or young woman from a neighboring
farm,—for there are no servants in the convention-

al sense—all are on a level among these country
folk. Of course we added the usual *douceur* to
our moderate bill ; but we heard afterwards that
the independent Norwegians prefer a trifling gift
in other shape, a gay-colored ribbon or a bright
handkerchief, accompanied by a pleasant word—
if one happens to know the word ! They always
acknowledge a gift of any kind by a shake of the
hand—a custom which, in the case of a cariole-
boy for instance, one would prefer " to honor in the
breach," for the hand of that personage, though,
like " the hand of Douglas," unquestionably " his
own," is not always immaculate. By a conver-
sion of genders the cariole-boy is sometimes a girl.
A little creature not more than nine years old
was in two instances deputed to sit behind on the
box and drive back the horse. No doubt it was
safe ; for the roads are good at this season, and the
animals are models of integrity.

After Fossegarden, noticeable for its fine cataract, the first station of interest was Kirkestuen, which boasts of a quaint little church containing some stiff Byzantine-like painted figures of Christ with angels, an almost solitary instance of such adornment in Norway. While we waited at the station to rest, a jolly old party, with great " breadth of beam" and a round face wreathed in smiles, stood still to be sketched, much to the delight of his family. I have no doubt he was the landlord ; and, in compliment to the Byzantine angels, he took an attitude as nearly as possible like theirs, rigid, ascetic, with pendent arms and monumental legs, as ludicrous a combination as could be imagined.

At the unpronounceably-named station of Skjaesggestad the dark red spire of another antique church is the only prominent object.

We passed the first night at the Listad farm, and astonished the hostess by asking for a separate room for each of the party. Such lack of sociability she could not comprehend ; but as she had no other guests, our persuasions prevailed, and we were soon ensconced in three enormous rooms, with a balcony looking upon sweet green fields framed in forest-covered hills. The air was delicious ; and supper, that important item to travellers, made savory by the sauce of good appetite, was served in a room decorated with pots of ivy which stood in corners whence the vines were trained over the walls quite to the ceiling. Sleep seemed an impertinence in that long opalescent twilight, followed, not by night, but by the sun ; and until he rose gayly at two o'clock the scene was more fitting for Romeo and Juliet than was that pent-up balcony overhanging the noisome street in Verona. Just then the fair Capulet of our party found herself quite happy without a Montague, but

" When enchantments afterwards befell "—

However, let us avoid personalities and resume our carioles!

The second day offered more variety than the first. Again the Laugen hurries its course, and forms farther on two cataracts which bound over rocks and sprinkle the fern-clad cliffs. Near Storklevestad is a house partly built of timbers which formed the one in which was born St. Olaf, one of the fierce evangelist - kings of the tenth century, whose title to saintship rests upon his destruction of the temples of Odin and Thor, and his propagation of the religion of peace by battle-axe and sword until his atrocities roused the whole country against him.

> " Norway never yet had seen
>    One so beautiful of mien,
>       One so royal in attire
>    When in arms completely furnished,
>    Harness gold-inlaid and burnished,
>       Mantle like a flame of fire.

. . . .

‘ I command
This land to be a Christian land ;
And if you ask me to restore
Your sacrifices, stained with gore,
Then will I offer human sacrifices—
Not slaves and peasants shall they be,
But men of note and high degree.’ ”

On and on runs the exhilarating river until it pauses to sleep in a small lake at Bredevaugen, but wakens again when reinforced by two torrents which are utilized to turn several saw-mills. These ordinarily uncouth structures do not mar the scenery in Norway, because the roofs are covered with green turf, and the pine logs lying about are harmonious with gray and yellow lichens.

We now pass a very steep hill called Kringelen, which was the scene in 1812 of the massacre of a number of Scotch troops under Colonel Sinclair, who had been despatched to assist Sweden in one of the numerous feuds between that country and its turbulent neighbor, Norway. In rashly attempting to pass through this valley to Sweden they were fatally surprised by about three hundred peasants, who hurled upon them from this hill an immense avalanche of rocks, stones, and roots of trees carefully collected for the purpose. A small monument and a tablet in the rock commemorate the disaster.

The road now rises gradually; the valley becomes dreary and desolate; there are no farmhouses for several miles through a desert of stones, sand, and *débris* from the mountains, whose only vegetation is stunted pines. The few laborers' cabins are roofed with birch-bark, covered with turf which is often prinked with bright flowers and occasionally affords footing for a small birchtree. A little farther on we reach the Rusten Pass, a magnificent gorge wooded thickly with firs and birches. The mountains nearly ap-

proach each other, the river forces its way
through precipitous rocks of gneiss, the air is filled
with spray of innumerable waterfalls from trickling threads to impetuous torrents, and the whole
scene is wild and grand in the extreme. At the
finest point of view we cross the ravine by a picturesque wooden bridge, about a hundred and fifty
feet above the foaming waters. We pass a pretty
church, in form of a Greek cross, entirely covered
with slabs of dark slate, and then reach Toftmoen,
which deserves mention as the abode of a descendant of Harald Haarfager (Harold of the
Fair Hair), who in 872 conquered and fused into
one the numerous small earldoms of Norway.
He had offered his warlike heart to a haughty
beauty named Gyda, who replied that she would
never marry the chief of a few insignificant provinces; only the throne of an absolute sovereign
would tempt her. To hear was to obey. The impetuous wooer registered a vow to Odin and all

the other gods that he would neither comb nor cut his hair until he had fairly won his suit, which he did at the decisive battle of Halfursfiord. The ambitious lady kept her promise, but history does not report whether she found herself happy in sharing her matrimonial honors with eight other wives, according to the custom of the period. Harald Haarfager's crown was by no means a comfortable ornament, for the dissatisfied provinces gave him endless trouble by their internal feuds ; but the Viking chiefs emigrated in large numbers, visited the entire sea-coast of Europe, made permanent homes in Scotland, Ireland, and Iceland, and even drifted to the shores of America. It was in the reign of this ancestor of Herr Toftmoen that the Viking ship previously mentioned was buried at Godstad. The lonely farm-house where we paused gives no external indication of royal lineage ; but the owner is considered passing rich, and keeps four hundred horses, two hundred sheep, and fifty goats in his stables all the winter.

When King Carl. XIII. stopped at this station to dine in 1860, on his way to Trondhjem to be crowned, the uncle of the present landlord sent word to his Majesty that it was unnecessary to unpack his travelling-case of silver, as there was quite enough in the house for the entire suite of forty persons; and when the dinner was served, this descendant of the Haarfager asserted his royal rank by dining also at the side of the king. The family pride runs in the blood still, though they are simple folk enough. One of them showed us some of their antique relics, which are used even now on proper occasions—a high silver wedding-crown, decked with colored stones but not jewels, which had rested on many a fair head in generations long past; silver chains, brooches, rings, and a girdle worn on the same occasions, some of which we wickedly coveted, as curios.

One of the sitting-rooms in this ancient house was dazzling to behold : a bright blue dado half-way up, and the remainder, together with the rafters, bright pale-yellow ! The pantries and closets were exhibited with housewifely pride, as well as an enormous key with most complicated wards which hung in the entrance-hall, souvenir of a past habitation. The boys of ten and twelve years who drove us to the next station were sons and heirs to this primitive wealth—frank, good-humored little chaps who amused themselves and us by repeating a few English words which seemed to them intensely funny. Their laughter was contagious, and we arrived in merry mood at 11 o'clock at Dombaas, our station for the night.

Eleven o'clock—only the edge of the evening in these high twilight-latitudes ! We met two gentlemen just sallying out for a walk ; cocks and hens were picking up vesper crumbs, and the house-dogs on hospitable *qui' vive* like the

master and the maids. And yet by four or five
the next morning all the household would be
astir. We often asked, " Do you never sleep in
summer?" "O, yes, but we *sleep* in winter,"—
implying that the brief, beautiful summer was for
*siesta* merely.

Any artificial light is of course out of the
question, and we rarely even saw a candle in
the bedrooms. As the windows have usually
only white muslin shades, the full blaze of the
sun, two or three hours after going to bed, in a
room where his evening reflections still lingered,
was more poetic than pleasing, and we were often
compelled to darken the windows with shawls
and rugs.

We had ascended from Toftmoen over great
stony barren plains to the plateau, two thousand
feet above the sea, on which stands the farm-house
of Herr Dombaas, externally bare and without
ornament of trees, but within doors the most at-

tractive of all the Norway stations. The intelligent and obliging landlord greeted us at the door in excellent English, which was a joy to our ears after two days of unmitigated Norsk. The entrance-hall was hung with white bear-skins and the pretty white fox-skins, the expressive heads undetached ; while above stretched the arms of fine branching antlers. The sitting-room had a very homelike aspect, with readable books and comfortable sofas. The air was pure and bracing, and we were very glad to repose in this pleasant place for two nights. Herr Dombaas owns one of the best *Sæters*, or mountain dairies, in Norway. In these sæters one may see life reduced to its primitive elements. They are rude log-cabins with the usual tiny roof, on mountain plateaux, sometimes three thousand feet high, to which in summer the farmers send two or three of their daughters with the cows and goats. The large room serves as sitting-room, bedroom, and kitchen. Those remaining form the dairy—all very clean, and the floors strewn, as they are in some parts of the farm-houses, with sweet-scented fir-branches. A writer in the *London Graphic* says: "There are two beds, and a belated traveller is always welcome to one of them ; for while purer-minded maidens do not exist than these mountain-lassies, there is no false modesty about them, nor have we ever heard of their hospitality being abused. No sooner does a traveller set foot inside of the door than one of them appears with a huge bowl of milk, of which it would be the greatest possible rudeness to refuse to partake. Of tips they are delightfully ignorant, but they thoroughly appreciate the gift of a bright-colored handkerchief or of a packet of English needles."

But while the life on these lonely mountains develops great simplicity and integrity of character, it is not surprising that traditions of the gnomes

who once mixed their weird loves and hates with
the impulses of humanity should still cast shadows
of superstition upon these primitive abodes ; and
we must be lenient to the fear of the sæter-maid,
who when her swain comes up for his Sunday
visit hopes he will not be ensnared on the way by
the Huldr, a tall fair woman in yellow bodice and
blue skirt, with golden hair flowing over her
shoulders, who sits on a rock, sewing or knitting,
for the malign purpose of stealing men's hearts
from their lawful owners.   Fortunately, the incessant toil of the dairy leaves little time for fancies ;
the milk of sheep, goats, and cows requires much
persuasion before it consents to assume its various
names.   The "gamle Ost," or old cheese, as
one quality becomes in course of time, might well
be omitted from the catalogue according to Anglo-Saxon ideas, for it salutes the olfactories in the
same overpowering way as the notorious Lim-
burger, and must be brought to the table in a

covered glass dish, which is as carefully opened as a bottle with a live reptile in.

The necessity for rest and letter-writing deprived us one day of a promised excursion on the Dovre Fjeld, the most famous of the mountain-ranges, and the one which separates Southern from Northern Norway. There are no well-defined chains as in Switzerland, and therefore no "passes," in the Swiss sense, but vast elevated plateaux, from which rise mountain-peaks sometimes to the height of eight thousand feet, and occasionally too precipitous for the snow to lie upon them. Above the range of the forests these plateaux are covered with stones and boulders disintegrated by frost. Of the Dovre Fjeld, Baedeker says : "A great part of the route traverses lofty, bleak, and treeless solitudes, rock-strewn tracts, swamps, gloomy lakes, and blackened masses of snow. The solemn grandeur of the scene, however, has a peculiar weird attraction of its own,

and the pure air is remarkably healthful and exhilarating." There is compensation even in these
desolate wastes to sportsmen, geologists, and botanists. Another writer speaks of the abundance
and variety of mosses and lichens clothing the
rocks with rich colors, and adds that after one
passes the crest of the Fjeld and descends to the
station of Kongsvold one finds it filled with Scandinavian botanists, who are attracted by the great
variety of Alpine flora. He says : " It is comical
to see detachments of professors and students
sallying forth in the early morning with their gayly-
colored tin cases slung around them. In the
afternoon they return laden with floral treasures
which they spread before the house on masses of
blotting-paper, kept from flying away by large
stones. Many, nay, most of these good people
can speak a little English, and when once the
natural reserve or shyness so characteristic of the
Norwegian is broken through, pleasanter or more

entertaining companions could scarcely be found."
We would gladly have looked upon the stern
heights which frown over the lovely valley we
had just passed, for everything in nature responds
to some experience or some imagination of
many-sided humanity ; but as we had permitted
ourselves the liberty of choice only, not of combination, this excursion was projected into some
shadowy by-and-by, and we turned our horses'
heads towards the more than compensating valley
of the Romsdal.

By the calendar that morning it was the 15th of
June : by the wind that blew down from the
snows of the Dovre Fjeld it was the 15th of De-
cember ; and the numerous warm wraps packed
for use in the Arctic Circle were all put in requisition. In fact, we never again found them so essential. But as we gradually descended, the cold
winds remained above, the mercury rose to its seasonable altitude, and the air was most exhilarating.

One must be prepared in Norway even more than in Switzerland for heat in the valleys and winter cold on the heights; but our experience found the temperature usually very equable. The day's drive was delightful, but not especially picturesque ; the Romsdal was still beyond sight, but we learned that for fishermen and huntsmen this region is a paradise. All the way from Lilliehamar the guide-books indicate *détours* for these healthful amusements and for mountain excursions. We had left the Lougen several miles behind, and as we neared Stueflatten, our station for the night, the road skirts the Rauma, which just presents itself in a narrow, precipitous ravine through which it tumbles in roaring haste. The solitary farm-house stands at the head of the gorge, and enjoys opportunities to "muse o'er flood and fell" that must be maddening when enforced the year round. It may have been this which had petrified the pretty girl who served our supper into a statue of sad

NORWEGIAN KITCHEN—STUEFLATTEN.

silence; not a muscle of her face moved in response to our admiration of the pale-yellow carnations in the window, or of the perfection of the "pankagen." I peeped into the quaint kitchen and asked permission to sketch the characteristic chimney. The whole household inspected as the work went on, and suggested snndry additions behind the foreground and beyond the linear perspective which if followed out would have compelled me to tear down a wall and make the drawing from the outside.

After the road leaves Stueflatten it descends by a series of rapid zigzags, and within a distance of seven miles there is a marvellous succession of beautiful waterfalls, some of them tumbling between perpendicular walls of basalt rocks until they culminate in the grand Slettefos. Here we alighted and crossed the river over a bridge of pine-logs to a ledge below the overhanging rocks, where the roar is loudly reverberated. "Flood

upon flood hurries on, never ending," of waters
lashed into foam between black ledges from which
fronds of fern and slender trees sway and quiver
in the sweep of the cataract. As we stood there, a
tiny hand holding a bunch of wild-flowers was
suddenly held before us—only a hand and nothing
more, till we turned and saw an elfin creature not
more than six years old, who had scrambled down
from a grassy knoll among the trees. Imagine a
life bounded by the cabin above and the torrent
below!

But we must pursue our road. Again and
again, fringes of silvery threads all adown the
stately hills! The rushing river sometimes pauses
to take breath, sometimes concentrates its foaming waters for mad leaps over stones and boulders ; the mountains on either side approach, again
they recede, once more they narrow the path, as
if petrified in some rhythmic measure, and here
at last we are in the valley of

# CHAPTER IV.

## THE ROMSDAL.

A LAS! already bankrupt in adjectives, my nouns and verbs tattered and torn with constant use, and the "courteous reader" yawning over the *débris*, I am sorely tempted to treat this new claimant in the happy manner of "The Snakes of Ireland"—There is *no* Romsdal valley in Norway! Yet I do indeed remember a panoramic dream of lofty pinnacles and serrated crags, four thousand to seven thousand feet high, fitly called the Witches' Peaks, baptized by waterfalls galore, foaming cataracts, and veils of finest spray which sparkle through dark pines and firs till they meet the river rushing through the curves of its rocky bed, mountains on either side closing the path at intervals as in a *cul-de-sac ;* and at last the Romsdalshorn, with sharply shattered summit, overtops and sentinels them all at the end of the valley. Then the mountains recede on either side; a broad green meadow flecked with purple violets sweeps towards the Romsdal fiord, and the Rauina, now transformed into the most peaceful of streams, glides towards the same goal.

At one point in this plain stands a large white house, formerly a hotel, but now the summer residence of an English gentleman. We afterwards met on a steamer several of his relatives who were invited there to pass the summer, making altogether a party of fourteen enviable people.

The road westward from this point runs through a charming park-like expanse supposed to be the covered and clothed remains of an old glacier moraine. The Romsdal fiord opens before us; the quaint village of Verblungnaes nestles upon it under the brow of a mountain. We preferred the station of Naes, as it commands a better view of the Romsdal range, and has the advantage of a new hotel in freer air. At ten o'clock at night we walked out to gather lilies of the valley, which grew in profusion thereabouts. The Trolltinderne, or "Witches' Peaks," uplifted fingers of fire towards the blue serene ; the Romsdalshorn, and yet loftier crests of the Vengetinder, glowed in crimson with deep purple shadows ; and the plaintive iteration of the cuckoo made the best of his limited minor thirds—a bird *incompris*, who is always moaning that the ideals of his heart are denied the expression of the gifted tenors and sopranos whose music

> " Bubbles, ripples up the dome
>    In sprays of silvery trilling ;
> Like endless fountain's lyric foam,
>    Still falling, still refilling."

The next day two of us drove back over a part of the Romsdal, to renew and deepen its impression. We walked in search of the finest points; we gazed, analyzed, compared, and then decided that we could *not* decide. Artists come there with canvas and colors, but the rich embarrassment mocks their selection.

The next morning, with Norwegian leisureliness, at seven o'clock we started on the steamer for Vestnaes, whence we were to post to Söholt. The fiord at first entrance looked like an inland lake, and the mountains around and behind gleamed in the morning sun with distinct individuality of form. The steamers on all these fiords not only cross and recross to opposite sides, but they also run into all the little tributaries where a hamlet or post-station exists, thus traversing a great deal of space and affording a good opportunity to scan the people. One sees many pretty hamlets nearly always under watch and ward of a white church on the hillside, and a cascade or two of more or less pretension. The steamer landed us at a grassy slope whence a shaded path led to the post-station, and our impedimenta followed after a long interval, under conduct of the only positively stupid boy we encountered in the journey.

At once we became the cynosure of a hundred eyes much enlarged for the occasion, belonging to a troop of Sunday-dressed boys and girls who were to be confirmed, though it was not Sunday, in the church near by. They crowded round us while we engaged vehicles for Söholt, the next station, but preserved a civil immobility of feature when our Norsk gave out disgracefully in certain unexpected exigencies. We obtained a cariole, but no trille was to be seen among the dozen dilapidated, unpainted, and extraordinary carts that were scattered about the premises ; for in Norway there are no sheds for vehicles outside of cities. So we were fain to put up with the novelty of a *Stælk-jærre*, a heavy springless cart seating two persons and a post-boy behind them. There was doubt

CHURCH IN GUDBRANSDAL.

about our obtaining even that, until there came
to the rescue the sister of the station-master, a
very conscious and smiling beauty, who must
have been the belle of the neighborhood, for she
was not only pretty, but well endowed in other
ways. She had learned "a few English" at
school in Molde, and not a few exotic graces.
Like the descendants of Harald Haarfager, the
family are pecuniarily independent and not over-
pleased to be subsidized by the government to entertain strangers. It is to be feared that at some
future time all this part of Norway may be ruined
by railways—and then, farewell forever to its
charm of simplicity and freshness. Already evil
spirits are suggesting one from Lilliehamar to the
western coast through the Gudbransdal and
Romsdal valleys; and the only salvation from such
a calamity lies in the fact that the foreign travel
is limited to about three months of the year, and
the commercial gain would be too trifling to com-

pensate the expense. Those who desire to see Norway before the army of summer locusts have devoured every green leaf of its honest forest-life would better go there as soon as may be, leaving behind all superfluity of dress and impatience of speech and manner. In truth, no one ought to visit it who does not worship nature more than fashion ; those who care only to roll from a Pullman car into a liveried hotel, to run through picture-galleries and buy diamonds,

> " to lord it o'er their fellow-men
> With most prevailing tinsel "—

will find no other welcome than

> " *Procul, procul, profani !* "

Our first trial of the springless stœlkjærre was happily our last. It was not a flowery bed of ease : the horse crept when the road was level, but dashed up hill and down hill with a vigor that left no doubt either of his own good intentions or of the consequences to ourselves. The happy individual in the cariole was not disturbed, but the tenants of the stœlkjærre have never solved the problem which was the largest factor in that drive, the misery or the mirth.

Very shortly after our first starting we passed a church with sloping, red-tiled roof where the boys and girls we encountered at the station were now receiving the rite of confirmation. This ceremony is compulsory and marks an important era in life, for no one can be married or obtain a situation in a factory or office before passing through it. The newspapers advertise for a "confirmed young man as clerk," or "a confirmed young woman as seamstress," etc. This is not a purely ecclesiastical observance as would be supposed, for it is preceded by at least six weeks' earnest instruction by the parish clergyman and his assistant, not only in theology but in many useful practical branches : examinations follow which must be satisfactory, or the pupil is remanded for another course. Confirmation is therefore a testimonial of a certain degree of knowledge and of good character. Both boys and girls are then supposed to be prepared for the duties of life. The religion is Lutheran, from which there is no dissent; it is partly under government control, at least so far as church property is concerned, for bishops and priests are maintained by funded revenues, and their widows and children provided for by a special appropriation. It is said that the Norwegians have great reverence and affection for their church, and that the clergy are remarkably intelligent and influential men. Some of them are members of Parliament, but not *ex officio*— merely as laymen.

Our road for several miles lay through smooth green plains, bright with wild-flowers, through which ran a little arm of the fiord that reflected

the log-cabins of the owners of the land ; then a
gay little torrent marked the way to a narrow valley, which gradually ascended to bare and treeless
mountains.  We changed horses at the only really
poor station we had seen, Ellengsgaard, a mere
peasant's dwelling, dirty and displeasing.  Happily we could dispense with food, and gladly
pushed onward through a very dreary region for
three hours, until we made an abrupt descent into
a sheltered valley where smiling vegetation, pleasant farms, and the blue Stor fiord indicated our
arrival at Söholt, a cluster, or rather a street, of
white and red houses that follows the shore and
offers all essential comforts to tourists in the new
and clean Alexandra hotel.  Supper and sleep
were very welcome that night after the early morning boat, the jolting stœlkjærre and the too-gen-
erous warmth of the sun.  The landlord of the
hostelry, named Ramussen, talks English fluently,
for he was a laborer six or seven years on an Illi-

nois farm, returned with his savings to "Gamle
Norge," built his inn, and then "they were married;" and we hope they will "live happily ever
after," for he is a good-hearted, honest son of the
soil who deserves to prosper. We were sympathetic with his pride in his new belongings, in his
store of household linen, and the new mattresses;
and when he asked us whether it was better to
leave the unpainted pine walls of some of the
chambers as they were or to paper them, we of
course voted against the paper.

The steamer, fettered by no horological laws,
was nearly two hours late the next morning.
After preliminary study of guide-books, gathering
of wild-flowers, and much discursive chat, we were
fain to betake ourselves to the one shop of the village to lay in a small stock of the national pipes
made of some dark polished wood, and soon
found ourselves the target of many feminine eyes,
which took in all the details of our dresses, and,

aided by fingers, even remarked with signal ap-
proval the confidential embroideries beneath.
At last the tardy steamer, with little to do and a
great deal of time to do it in, puffed around the
promontory, and we were soon ensconced for the
next ten hours in a favorable position for studying
the fiord and its confluents.   The views were very
varied, of green meadows with background of
mountains traversed by the inevitable waterfalls,
uplying farms, tiny red hamlets on the shore,
quaint-looking people, and fishermen in quiet
nooks, with their log-houses perched on ledges of
the cliffs.   We crossed and recrossed continually,
taking on and putting off cargo, and parties of
peasants who were a study in manners and dress.
There are no very distinctive costumes here as in
some other parts of Norway; the men wear very
loose, one might almost say *flowing*, coats, short
waistcoats, gay neckties, and high felt hats when
in "full dress"—ordinarily they dispense with a

coat; the women wear short dark woollen skirts, white bodies, bright or white handkerchiefs on their heads, and silver brooches and chains of antique make. A large wedding-party came on board in this attire and with an air of solemnity that included even the violinist, who appeared much more ready for an epitaph than an epithalamium. The bride was not of the number; and the groom, a stalwart young fellow in brown coat and scarlet cravat, soon found himself unequal to the embarrassing occasion and shyly retired out of sight. When the landing-point was reached he reappeared, full of care for certain barrels which he and his "best man" rolled on shore, containing, we were told, supplies for the wedding-feast, beer, fladbrod, cheese, and sweet cakes. Several quiet cheers and exclamations of *"God Held!"* ("Good luck!") saluted their departure; and we waved our handkerchiefs, wishing that we had an invitation to the ceremony. The party was to pro-

ceed to the home of the bride, two or three miles
distant, and the festivities, lasting three days, would
begin on their arrival.  The marriage takes place
at the church always on Sunday ;  each guest brings
a present, and the bride wears the silver girdle
and frontlet and the high silver crown which in-
vests every Norwegian girl with queenly honors
for one day in her life, and then these ornaments
are laid away until another bride comes to claim
them.  Another party landed to attend a protracted religious meeting in which fasting was not
a feature, as they also were furnished with barrels
of provisions.  The trunks and boxes that came
and went were curiosities for a museum.  They
were usually painted in bright colors, such as a
dark-blue ground with red and yellow flowers, to
which the dates were added :  we noticed one
dated 1782, and another still fit for service revealed
a world of domestic contentment in the figures
1689!

As we proceeded down the Nord fiord the mountains became higher and more imposing, until the steamer turned almost at right angles into that superb water-defile, the Geiranger fiord, which one writer pronounces the "culmination of all the fiords of that region, its only rival in Norway, perhaps in the world, being the Nero fiord, which it resembles." Its dark, unmeasured depths are walled by rocky cliffs, often perpendicular, which rise to the height of three thousand to four thousand feet. Countless light, gauzy waterfalls descend from their summits, often uniting in one roaring mass ; stunted firs and birches cling wherever their roots can find support, and adventurous flowers sway from the crevices. Our liquid path is so narrow and the curves so abrupt that the steamer sometimes appears to be running sharply against the rocks, while the spray of the falls bathes it in a gentle shower. When winter reigns supreme, avalanches of snow and stones thunder

GEIRANGER FIORD.

down from these majestic bastions, whose tops are never touched by the sun, except for a brief hour or two at high noon. And yet in this awful solitude a few human beings live and move and preserve their being. We saw two cabins on different mountains, almost overhanging the ledge like eagles' nests. The small grassy plateaux on which they stand are at least two thousand feet from the black flood below ; an apparently perpendicular path and a tiny boat forming the only means of communication with the world. A cow that grazes on the mountain-top, and perhaps a couple of goats, furnish milk. Goats and babies are tethered to the threshold or the rocks, but adults have occasionally by a fatal misstep been precipitated,

> " Low and lower, to their watery graves,
> With downward face and wide-spread hair!"

When a death occurs in winter, the body is laid away in snow until the return of spring permits interment in the nearest village cemetery. It is inconceivable that all the fulness of our generous planet should offer nothing but this perilous, desolate scrap of earth to these poor families. They possess, to be sure, the rare boon of pure air and unadulterated food, such as it is, and would doubtless answer our fretful inquiry, "Is life worth living?" from a standpoint very remote from ours; but we, from the plane below, recalled the remark of Théophile Gautier when visiting the Escorial: "Whenever hereafter I find myself bored or unhappy, I shall be consoled in remembering that I *might* be at the Escorial and that I am *not* there." On the whole, for a short stay the hut on the Geiranger would seem to me preferable.

Only an hour is required for the *traversée* of this unique defile ; the steamer stops half an hour at Merak, the village at the end, and the return through the fiord imprints every detail on the memory. There are many beautiful excursions from Merak ; in fact, the guide-books teem with alluring invitations to by-ways as well as high-ways all through the Scandinavian peninsula.

Emerging from the Geiranger, the boat crossed to Hellesylt, the village where we intended to pass the night. We made our way up a rough, stony path to as primitive an inn as can well be seen, to find it so crowded ("crowd" implying about two dozen people) that we gladly returned to the steamer, which the captain had previously warned us would be more comfortable. He received us with a friendly laugh and with Spanish hospitality : " I *thought* you would come back, ladies! Now the boat shall all be yours, to-night—only give me my cabin." We were put in possession of the dining-saloon, with the small ladies' cabin for a dressing-room ; we had blankets and pillows *ad libitum;* and when six o'clock came the next morn-ing were still sleeping undisturbed by the hasty toilet, the bill, and the rush to the boat which preluded the breakfast of our fellow-travellers. The weather was dull, and the wind fresh ; the steamer again crowded with peasants coming and going, and there was no first-class deck. Again the good captain came to our aid and gave us his own cabin, where with wraps and rugs we had a retrospect of the Nord fiord, increased in interest by his traditions of the rocks and stories of the people, recounted in fair English. The mate was equally entertaining, and very proud of his three visits to the United States. "O yes," he said in reply to some encouraging remark, " I like New York ; I lived in a fine street there—Pearl Street. You know Pearl Street? And I have been to Chicago, too ; I was there when the great fire was. I want to go back again. O yes, if I live I shall see New York again before I die." For the sake of our nationality he kept watch and ward over our audience-room, and banished the inquisitive boys and girls who peeped in at the

door as if we were the royal animals of a menag-
erie ; and when we left the steamer on arriving at
Aalesund on the western coast, our trifling gratuity, accompanied by the gift of a purse from the
city of his admiration, brought tears to his eyes.
Norwegians usually receive good impressions of
our country from their emigrating compatriots ;
many of the seamen and skippers have sailed to
and from our shores, and have brought back a
slight knowledge of the language and reminis-
cences of wonderful fruits, grand buildings, gala
spectacles, and a general gorgeousness, such as
the palaces of Bagdad offered to the dazzled eyes
of Aladdin.

We had several unemployed hours to spare at
Aalesund before the arrival of the steamer for
Molde, our next halting-place, and we improved
this interval by rambling about the town. Although a small place of only six or seven thousand inhabitants, it is one of the principal sea-

ports, and renowned for its good pilots, hardy fishermen, and codfishery. As Mark Twain said of Bermuda, "its pride and its joy, its gem and its jewel, is the Onion," so of Aalesund its gem and its jewel is the Cod, whose mortal remains pervade the atmosphere with undeniable conviction. Italy and Spain are its final destination as a noun of multitude. When religious fast-days vanish from that part of the world in the progress of ages, Aalesund will no longer find these so generous marts for her codfish. Meanwhile Spain returns a more savory freight in excellent port-wine, which finds its way at moderate prices all over Norway. The town lies partly on the main-land and partly on islands, thus affording to imaginative travellers a likeness to Venice. Two or three water-ways and bridges can never come together without the immediate exclamation "Venice!" as if prototype or semblance of the unique beauty of that peerless city ever yet existed anywhere! Behind the town rises a huge cliff from which the sunset shining on the sea, and the fringe of islands off the coast, would be the delight and the despair of an artist. The streets are neither quaint nor old, but there is one historical relic—the ancient castle of "Hrolf Gangr," or Rollo the Walker, so called because, on account of his great height and size, no Norwegian horse could carry him. He was the conqueror and founder of the duchy of Normandy, the progenitor of William the Conqueror, and of the same mould and spirit as that race of Normans and Norsemen united who subjugated Sicily and inwove the iron threads of Scandinavian energy into the golden tissue of Arabic and Greek refinement. The country around Aalesund teems with traditions of the Sea-Kings who from this favorite point set their square sails and lofty prows in search of far-off Pactolian streams.

We started on our voyage for Molde about

eight in the evening, and arrived there at two in the morning, after spending nearly all the interval in chatting on the deck with chance acquaintances. These June· nights-which-are-not-nights seem to steal the pivot from the wheel of Time, and our watches formed the habit of incorrigible lying. One o'clock, they say—and a pink and primrose sky flatly contradicts ; two o'oclock—a rosier gold, and lo, the sun ! No chronometer in the world could stand such *bouleversement.*

Molde is a clean, pretty town of two thousand inhabitants, and is more favored in climate than most others in Norway, for it stands on the western coast, under the influence of the Gulf Stream, and is sheltered from north winds by a range of hills. Flowers both wild and cultivated grow in abundance—roses, anemones, honeysuckles, butterfly-orchids, and many others. It boasts attractive villas and gardens, and charming walks up the hills, whence stretches

an extensive panorama of the fiord with its
many islands, and, beyond, snow-tipped mountains which recall the Bernese Alps as seen from
the Schäuzli. The new and excellent Grand
Hotel, with its baths, balconies, and admirable
*cuisine*, would have tempted us to many days' so-
journ had not inexorable Fate waved in her hand
our tickets, marked June 23, for the *Capella*,
bound to the North Cape. No choice was left,
and we embarked again at midnight on our sixth
steamer.

# CHAPTER V.

THESE fiord steamers have a fashion of starting at such times as anywhere else would
be objectionable ; but when the days are twenty-
four hours long, one hour is as good as another.

A few hours' sleep in comfortable cabins tided
us kindly over the somewhat emotional open sea
which sweeps around the coast, not always sheltered by the breakwater of islands. We paused
at Christiansund "for cargo" as usual, but readily
restrained our curiosity to see it, except from our
cabin windows, as it has no interest for travellers.
It is built with singular irregularity on three islands ; there is nothing outside but the sea and
barren rocks, and little inside except the . multi-

tudinous cod. Beyond this point the scenery is rather picturesque. We sat on deck in view of friendly islands, and soon entered the extensive fiord of Trondhjem. *En passant* it may be said that all these fiord steamers provide an abundance of good food and good sleeping-cabins—which latter, however, are few in number and ought to be engaged at least two or three days in advance by telegram or letter to the main offices. There is a curious custom of asking for families what they call a " moderation " price, which means that a man and his wife, or a brother and sister, pay for only one and a half tickets. This explains the title of a pleasant little book called " One and a Half in Norway."

I have not hitherto trenched on the province of the guide-books by mentioning prices, but it may be well to state here that the cost of travelling is about five dollars per day, including steamer-fares, cariole or trille, meals and beds. In the three large cities, Bergen, Christiania, and Trondhjem, hotel-prices are much the same as in Switzerland and Germany. Railways are few, and for those who have time the post-roads are preferable, especially considering the facilities they constantly offer for *détours* into regions of grandeur and beauty necessarily shunned by the iron road. One hears of many discomforts in what are called the "slow stations"—that is, where tourists are few and farmers have only two or three horses and poor accommodations; but to see as well as to be the beautiful,—" *il faut souffrir.*"

I am again impelled to laud the friendly, obliging civility of the Norwegians ; and as to honesty, Diogenes might throw away his lamp, for his honest man is the universal man, woman, and child. Scarcely any crime is considered so disgraceful as dishonesty. An Englishwoman who had lived twenty-six years in Christiania said to us: "If you should fill this room with gold coins and send a

Norwegian into it alone, he would not touch a
single piece." Linen may be left on the grass all
night to bleach ; trinkets and watches are safe on
bedroom tables with doors unlocked ; and both
purses and watches lost on the roads are taken to
the nearest inn. This delightful trait includes
honesty of speech and of deed, and is the nearest
approach to the window in the heart which the
satirist of Olympus declared wanting in Vulcan's
primeval man. One remembers with indignation
the extortions formerly practised upon some of
these unsophisticated emigrants in the great port
of New York ; happily they are now much better
protected : but in a country where peculations and
falsehoods fly like thistle-down through the air,
eternal vigilance is the price of justice.

TRONDHJEM,

the home of the Thrones, an important tribe
of olden days, has always been the historical

capital, and the sovereigns of the United Kingdom are still crowned there in the cathedral. The approach is picturesque by both land and water; the town, numbering thirty thousand inhabitants, lies on a peninsula formed by the river Nid on

IN TRONDHJEM CATHEDRAL.

one side and the fiord on the other; beyond are distant hills and the remains of a fort. The harbor is gay with ships of every sort, especially the *Jægts*, or copies of the Viking craft, with the same high prows and almost unaltered lines of their prototypes; and the quays are lined with dark-red

warehouses which extend into the water on piles,
as in Holland.

We had secured good rooms in the Britannia
Hotel, where baths and beds were very welcome
after three successive nights in steamers, as was
also the well-prepared and well-served dinner
in a pretty dining-room of carved wood from
floor to rafters.   The scene was animated by forty
or fifty polyglot guests, among whom were half
a dozen of our compatriots, and an elderly Englishman whose volcanic cynicisms had amused
us all the morning on the steamer.   We went out
after dinner for a survey of the city.   As in all
the other towns, the architecture is strikingly simple, the houses being generally of wood and rarely
more than two stories high ; the streets very broad
and regular, and the churches without spires.
Except on the quays and the market-place, there
is an orderly stillness ; and the general aspect of
the yellowish-gray houses would be dull but for

the pots of gay flowers that brighten every window.

I confess to the full amount of feminine interest in the shops of arctic furs and antique silver.
There is really but one for furs, and that is
Braun's, where we expected to find them better and
less expensive than anywhere else, unless in Russia.    But seal-skins cost very little less than in
England, and silver-fox and sables were so dear
that we reserved our purchases for their native
country.    We bought, however, unusually. dark
and beautiful Russian squirrel-robes at half the
price they cost elsewhere.    The antique silver goblets were very unique and finely engraved, and one
proved irresistible.    Among the spoons, not more
than half a dozen tempted to purchase ; they cost
from four to sixteen dollars—sixteen to seventy-
five "kroner."    Those worth buying are now very
scarce, most of them having taken Horace Gree-
ley's advice and "gone West."    Modern filigree

work is well done and very pretty ; the art of making it was learned from two Genoese who strayed hither two hundred years ago. It is, however, scarcely so fine as the Italian.

There is no prominent street of shops ; they modestly occupy the first floor of dwellings, and are small and unpretending. There are several attractive drives in the neighborhood of Trondhjem, one or two *soi-disant* gardens in the city, and a general air of comfort and content among the people. Prosperity is indicated by the ship-building yards, paper-mills, and other manufactories, besides the exports of timber, fish, and copper from the mines of Röras, which have been worked two hundred and fifty years ; and, singularly enough, cargoes of paving-stones have lately been sent to the city of New York !

The pride of Trondhjem and of all Norway is the cathedral, which was begun in the tenth century and was a hundred years in process of build-

APSE OF ST. OLAF'S CATHEDRAL.

ing—a really beautiful specimen of the massive
Norman and early English architecture, and, in
spite of certain later disfigurements, considered
the finest church in the three Scandinavian countries. This ancient pile stands a little apart, in a
well-kept church-yard, among such shrubs and
flowers as the climate affords. It is built of a
bluish slate which contrasts well with white marble columns in the interior; near the high altar
stands a replica of Thorwaldsen's majestic Christ,
presented by the sculptor, the effect of which is
very noble as seen from the entrance-door. The
favorite Saint Olaf was buried here; his shrine became a Mecca of the Catholic world, who enriched
it with magnificent gifts, supplanted the temples
of Odin with churches and monasteries, and
brought great prosperity to Trondhjem, until the
crusaders of the Reformation, in their turn, swept
away the monasteries, sacked the shrine, and
packed its gold and jewels in a ship which after-

wards foundered at sea. This was the beginning
of many disasters ; several conflagrations and the
pestilence of the "Black Death" nearly annihi-
lated the unhappy town until, about a hundred
years ago, it struggled into life again, and now
holds its own right valiantly, encouraged also by
the railways to Christiania and to Stockholm.

We were a jubilant party at Trondhjem, proud
of our punctuality and our strict adherence to our
chart of travel ; happy that no personal accident
or failure of any kind had barred our way. As
the fiord steamers ply only on certain days, which
are frequently changed, the delay of a single day
might have entailed the loss of our rooms on the
*Capella.* But here we were, within twenty-four
hours' sail of that Arctic Ocean which we had so
often traversed in fancy, and, turning away from
the generous but unsufficing Past, we lifted eager
eyes towards that anomalous meridian which
marks the fusion of day with immediate day again.

# CHAPTER VI.

## THE ARCTIC OCEAN.

THE first tourist steamer of the season had sailed June 21st; the *Capella*, of three days later, considered even better, lay in the harbor awaiting its freight of forty passengers. It had good cabins, a good *cuisine*, and excellent officers. Captain Iveson, a handsome, comfortable-looking man, won our hearts by his first act of courtesy. The only two cabins which we were able to secure two weeks previously proved uncomfortably small for a party of three, and with dismay in our hearts we applied to him for another. One large cabin remained disengaged, but that one, he said, might have been secured at Bergen; he could not tell until the passenger-list should arrive that day. Here was the first *contretemps* of our tour, and we were apprehensive of very crowded quarters during our eight days' voyage.

" Give yourselves no anxiety, ladies," said this most gracious of ship-masters ; " if there is no other cabin, I will give you mine."

We assured him we would gladly indemnify him for the sacrifice,—his cabin was the largest and best on the steamer,—but he would not listen to this proposal, and said he had given it away many a time. Happily the necessity was avoided, as no new passengers appeared at the last moment. I will say *en passant* that it is best to secure tickets two or three weeks, at least, in advance from the main office at Bergen ; not knowing this, we had bought ours at Christiania when all the best cabins assigned to that office had already been disposed of. The prices are from fourteen to fifteen pounds sterling, everything included. On all but the tourist steamers meals are not included.

We went on board at midnight, in the pink and purple hour between two days. A crowd stood on shore to watch the departure. "Farvels" rang through the air, handkerchiefs waved, the anchor was raised, and with a resolute purpose in her heart our *Capella* started for the land of the Midnight Sun.

We watched the little city with its hills receding and the islands approaching; we reviewed our fellow-passengers as they walked the deck in the self-gratulation of a fresh departure, and we cast our social horoscope with the usual quick, furtive observation of prospective comrades on a sea-voyage. Our forty passengers made a desirable number for comfort on the *Capella*, though it has carried a hundred and twenty. There were about a dozen English and Americans; the remainder were Danes, Swedes, Germans, Russians, and one

elderly Italian, whose only vocabulary was as use-
less as Patagonian in Norway, but who managed
with his unfailing good-humor and the ægis of
Cook's tickets to be sent forward like an express
parcel well labelled. At the table we were seated
next the captain, and our ears had the inestimable
privilege of hearing four unknown languages at
the same time from our opposite neighbors—a
Russian general, courtly and decisive ; a member
of the Swedish parliament, ponderous and solemn ;
a professor from Upsala University, with flowing
locks and a fair, sprightly wife ; and, as the fourth
in this bewildering fugue, a Dane, whose incessant
chatter never ceased during the entire voyage.

Our first day from Trondhjem presented no very
striking scenery. We were first in the Trondhjem
fiord, and afterwards in a network of islands, the
cliffs and rocks of which are not lofty, and have
no salient features except the bare and broken
contortions produced by the action of ice and

snow. Sometimes we pass into what appears a large lake, with innumerable little bays and armlets running into the fissures of the mountains; again the channel narrows and dark ledges of snow-tipped rock stretch across it. Even in July fogs and sleet often envelop this coast with dreary mantle ; but now the delightful air, the dreamy perspectives, and fair promise of both barometer and thermometer left nothing to desire. A few clouds hovered around, which awakened a little anxiety lest they should veil our first view of the midnight sun ; but as the day wore on they kindly drifted above the horizon.

During the entire voyage the weather was so calm that there was no question of discussion between digestion and dinner with even the most sensitive *voyageur*, and every day we went on shore to see some point of interest. The business of the ship was to entertain the passengers ; and as we fell in with the unique amusements thus presented, and also formed friendly alliances with our neighbors, the excursion soon took on the semblance of a private yachting-party.

We landed the first day on an island named Torgnet, which is surmounted by a lofty, precipitous rock called Torghætten, from its fancied likeness to a colossal hat or hood. The rock is about a thousand feet high, and perforated in the centre by a natural tunnel or cavern through which appears, as a picture in a gigantic frame, the sky and a group of islands on the other side. This remarkable orifice is five hundred feet up the rock, and one of the amusements of the voyage is to scramble up and look through it. After a few hundred yards over a flower-sprent, marshy meadow, the ascent is rough and steep, up and over great stones and *débris*, and through pools of water. At the edge of the cavern we came upon a group of fresh-checked peasant-girls in white bodices and gay handkerchiefs, offering photographs and bowls of milk. I was very grateful in that toilsome path for the aid of the first officer, a Scandinavian Adonis with beautiful, clear coloring, and kindly ways, always ready to act the part of *preux cheva-lier* to ladies young and old.

Of course a tragic legend is attached to this striking freak of nature, the Torghætten, for through all this stern and rugged coast superstition naturally takes that form. The story here is much like that of Daphne pursued by Apollo, with a Nemesis thrown in, and the persons of the drama stand in perpetual stone.

After resuming our voyage, the mountains on either side soon become very imposing, especially a range of seven weird peaks three thousand feet high, called the Seven Sisters, which, according to traditions of the Finns, the first inhabitants of Norway, are the homes of spirits hostile to all their successors. Farther on is a wonderful mountain called the Hestemand (Horseman), which by aid of imagination becomes a flying rider with wide-extended mantle, crags and cliffs representing the head of his steed and his own hand. Next appears on our fast-changing panorama the vast glacier of the Svartis, hundreds of square miles in area, which covers a plateau four thousand feet high and sends several of its jagged spurs quite down to the sea.

Soon after the captain summons us with the electric words, "Now, ladies and gentlemen, we are entering the Arctic Circle;" and, executing a gay little *pas-seul* on the centre of the deck, he stretches a rope firmly across to represent the line that divides us from the zone we leave behind. "You must be on duty till two o'clock," he adds; "no one is allowed to go to bed: there is too much to see; and coffee will be served on deck at twelve." For the first time we were far enough northward to see the sun at that mystic hour. All the day we had anxiously watched barometer and clouds. In truth they threatened disappointment, until about half-past eleven at night—night was Day, for we passed from light to Light—and then we beheld a marvel of a sunset.

Over the vast dome, almost to the zenith, the gray cloud-masses floated away in long fleecy scrolls of crimson and orange, in feathery filaments of transparent radiance, in downy flecks of deep purple edged with gold. Points and peaks both of mountains and clouds, in infinite irregularities, "with sunfire garlanded," sentinelled the sea, and stretched far northward till lost in translucent mist. Sea-birds disported themselves on the flashing waves, their sombre feathers transmuted to tropical iridescence. The sun slowly descended to the edge of the horizon;—and then, with one kiss on the radiant water, *rose* with elastic rebound! The dying and the new-born day clasp hands in mutual embrace as they pass through the duplicate golden portal; every ripple is a jewelled witness, every quiver of air an echo, of the celestial drama.

The beauty and the marvel of the scene brought silence upon all our little company; each one seemed afraid to speak lest he should break the spell, until, by imperceptible gradations of form and hue, the clouds were again lost in full blaze of light.

Then we were summoned to our *café au lait*, a little weary of the kaleidoscopic views of the long day, but reluctant even then to lose any hours in sleep. In truth we lost very few, for the steamers arrange so as not to pass the salient points during sleeping-hours—that is, from one o'clock in the morning until seven or eight. Some of the passengers never lost more than four or five hours; others remained on deck, wrapped in rugs and ulsters, dreamily gazing through the filmy smoke of their cigars at the ever-shifting peaks and promontories, glaciers and waterfalls, hamlets, fishing-

boats and ships, blue in shadow, but glistening in
the peculiar mellow light of that northern sea.
Sometimes they would waken from a half-con-
scious nap to see close upon the *Capella's* bows a
huge Viking ship, a ghost of ten centuries ago
returned to look for its comrades—not, however,
bristling with battle-axe and shields, but freighted
with freshly-cut timber and highly realistic cod and
herring. Murray says of these *Jægls :* "So pre-
judiced are the people who build and navigate
them that they will not make the slightest altera-
tion in their build or rig ; they will not even avail
themselves of the use of the windlass, so that the
huge square sail requires the same power to haul
it to the mast-head that it did twelve hundred
years since ; and for the same reason the anchor
has to be supplied with a special tripping to cant
it before it can be lifted. Many are now carvel-
built, but until recently they were all clinker-built,
with great breadth of beam and small draught of

water, enabling them to sail very fast before the
wind, but in beating they are apt to fall to lee-
ward."

The first coaling-point touched by the steamer
was Bodöe, a village of fifteen hundred inhabitants,
endowed with a telegraph-station, but not sufficiently interesting to tempt us to go on shore;
though if one had time and inclination, the excursions from these lead into the very heart of all
that is most wild and stern in Norway, especially
among the Lofoden islands, which we passed
very soon after Bodöe.   They form a remarkable
maze of red granite cliffs, bays, and narrow straits,
interspersed with thousands of rocky islands,
forming a chain one hundred and thirty miles
long.   Some of them have the appearance of volcanic craters, and are so sharply indented that they
are compared to the jaw of a great shark, with
its projecting teeth.   Snow-peaks and glaciers lie
among them, and a touch of life is given by fish-

ermen's huts and flocks of sea-birds. Among these straits are many dangerous currents, especially the Maelström, which formerly we were taught was a horrible whirlpool sure to engulf every object that comes near it. Though this is now pronounced a fable, the fact remains that when the wind blows from the northwest and meets the returning tide in the strait, the whole area of the Maelström becomes so turbulent that no ship could live in it for a moment, although outside the sea may be as still as glass. To add to the danger, the depth of the bottom very suddenly decreases and the whole weight of water from the North Sea is suddenly compressed between the two cliffs that form the strait ; a ship must therefore inevitably strike on sunken rocks or founder in the fury of the waves. There is another very narrow inlet near the Maelström into which unwary whales occasionally stray, and finding it impossible to turn their huge bodies, they are grounded with the falling tide, and sometimes struggle with their fate several days before dying in this natural trap, while the coast resounds with their bellowings and struggles. A large fortune is not often so vehemently thrust upon a man as it was in the case of a farmer who owned the land adjacent to this strait and became in a few years legatee of about twenty of these valuable cetaceans, whereupon he was dubbed with the title of King of the Lofoden Islands.

We did not steer within sight of these fatal currents, and our best view of the islands was on our return voyage, when we ran close to their base. The gigantic rocks rising almost perpendicularly from the sea are gnarled, twisted, and rent in every imaginable form, and the snow on their tops contrasts vividly with a remarkable green and yellow moss that grows in large patches upon them, and looks at a distance like a luminous field of opal and gold. The waters here, as on the entire coast, may be called the life-blood of Norway; from January to April about twenty thousand men are engaged in the Lofoden fishing for cod. They are a brave and temperate race, who suffer great hardships in the winter, especially from the northwesterly gales, which often drive their boats into open seas, where they inevitably capsize. But the climate is on the whole so tempered by the Gulf Stream that even this part of Norway is pleasantly habitable, while Greenland, in the same latitude (about 67°), is a desert of ice. If this beneficent river should take a new departure, the fish would emigrate,—and then so must the people, or starve.

The once busy town of Tromsöe, where we landed the second morning after leaving Trondhjem, has fallen off seriously within a few years on account of a freak on the part of the fish, which for reasons unknown have nearly deserted that locality. We went on shore at Tromsöe,

which is the principal settlement within the Arctic
Circle, built on a green, well-wooded island, and
enjoying a milder climate than most of the coast.
Nothing could be more severely simple than the
"Cathedral" (one of the rarely-seen Catholic
churches of Norway), the bank, the school-
houses, and the red-roofed dwellings. We went
into several shops of furs of various sorts, in rugs,
overcoats, and ladies' cloaks, insupportably heavy ;
also white fur shoes trimmed with red cloth made
by the Lapps. Several of these queer little nomads were bargaining for exchange of products,
and regarded us with more good-humor than curiosity, for they are accustomed to the sight of summer visitors. We strayed into a small museum
and examined a natural-history department of
fishes and animals peculiar to that region, but
all of which we had seen in other collections.
Another room was devoted to objects used by the
Laplanders—weapons, ornaments, clothing, etc.,

rather barbaric, but not lacking picturesqueness. In a small collection of coins we were surprised to see a ten-cent bit of United States paper currency, a "One Dollar" note, and two Confederate notes of *soi-disant* high value.

The birch trees of Tromsöe are rather fine for that latitude; wild-flowers, such as pale violets, heather, and buttercups, make a pathetic effort to represent summer, and pots of geraniums appear in every window. Fruits and vegetables of course refuse to grow. The first officer told us that he had spent a winter there, and although they could dispense with lamps only five or six hours of the twenty-four, the nights were enlivened by dances, music, and theatricals, and altogether it was social and agreeable. The Aurora Borealis is a most kindly alleviation of those interminable months, and must be almost as well worth seeing as the Midnight Sun. Two oil-paintings of it hung outside of a shop-window which we passed, and though they represented an apparently supernatural gorgeousness of color, our friend assured us they did not exaggerate.

This part of Norway is called Finmark, and from here to the North Coast of Scandinavia and Russia roam those dwellers in tents called Finns and Lapps. Once masters of the whole peninsula, they have been gradually driven to the bleak and desolate mountains, where they exist with their reindeer in a state of perennial contentment—a frame of mind either appertinent to nomads who have become an integral part of Nature itself, or attained after a severe struggle against the "divine despair" of high civilization. Some of the Norwegian Lapps come down to the valleys near Tromsöe in the summer season for the pasturage and fishing, and travellers usually visit their encampment.

The steamer sent us in boats to the shore, where horses were waiting for those who preferred the saddle to the walk of two miles in a charming birch-forest, through which ran a bustling rivulet. The air was perfect, the sky true blue, and the brief change from deck to shore very agreeable. As we approached the encampment which lay at the foot of green mountains, we saw a few hundred reindeer inclosed within a rude picket of tree-branches, several circular huts, and forty or fifty uncouth-looking men, women, and children, nearly all with pipes in their mouths. Nature has not been gracious to this tribe : she has stunted their stature to four and five feet, and has given them high cheek-bones, flat noses, thick, wide mouths, and swarthy skins, inharmonious with small blue eyes, to which they add long, unkempt brown hair. Even the babies looked old and smoke-dried, and the old people as shrivelled as mummies. But the good-humor of their faces goes a long way towards atonement. When we declined to buy their fur shoes and reindeer-horn

LAPLANDER.

spoons, they smiled as imperturbably as a Parisian shop-keeper. However, we bestowed small coins, and regretted, as usual, that we had no gay barbaric trifles to give them, or the more useful boon of coarse needles for the women. The men wore loose tunics of reindeer-skin, often sadly destitute of hair and sometimes made on the reverse side, fastened round the waist with belts, to which knives and tobacco-pouches were attached; peaked boots or shoes of reindeer-skin, the fur outwards and trimmed, as were their leggings, with bright red or blue woollen cloth ; pointed caps of red or blue wool surmounted their elfin locks. The women were clad in short, bright-colored woollen skirts, to which smoke and dirt had added a tint or two, and reindeer jackets so adjusted as to show rather lavishly the scraggy brown throat decked with silver ornaments. True to the undying instinct of the sex, they regarded our dress with curiosity, and probably were disappointed in the quiet hues ; but the gift to one young woman of a red-satin bow taken from a parasol was rap-

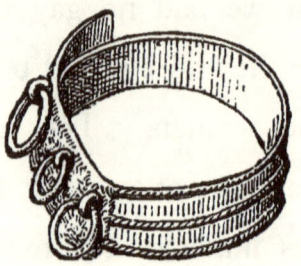

turously received and thrust for safe-keeping into her bosom, as a treasure not to be lightly displayed.    The hands  of  both  men  and

LAPP WEDDING-RING.    women would puzzle Des-

barolles; they are remarkably small and well-shaped, with almost "artistic" fingers.

We received ready admission into one of their *Gammer*, or huts, through an inconveniently low entrance, which was closed with a reindeer-skin. It was not more than eight feet in diameter, built of birch-bark supported on saplings, and filled in with earth ; the walls inside hung with deer-skins, wooden bowls, cheese, dried meat, guns ; and in one corner was a chest, probably for holiday clothing.    In the centre was a fire, and a kettle hung over the embers ; a very young Lapp, hideous as a monkey, lay choking in the smoke, and several other scions of the family toddled almost into the *pot au feu*, while at least three women endeavored to do the honors of the mansion.

The limitations of such a life are inconceivable, when we learn that these people know how to read and write after a fashion, and say their prayers devoutly in Lutheran churches when the opportunity offers. There are itinerant schoolmasters who instruct them a few weeks in the summer, employed by the government at the exorbitant rate of twenty-five dollars the season, the colony of Lapps contributing five dollars more; and we noticed at Hammerfest on Sunday several Lapps in the little church we visited. They were gross idolaters, however, until in 1600 A.D. Christian IV. of Denmark and Norway broke up their worship with great severity. The most vehement and fanatical preachers are the most popular with them—and there are many such in Nor-

way.   Nevertheless the dust of ancient superstitions still clings to their feeble brains ; they believe in witchcraft and in the Troller, or evil spirits
of the woods, and maintain the legendary supe-
riority of the polar bear as the most gifted of
created beings, capable of hearing and resenting
all disrespectful remarks that may be made about
him.   They are quite willing to destroy him, but
never when he is asleep — only with honorable
warning and an honorable weapon, such as a
lance—never a gun.   It is recorded that formerly
they asked his pardon with tears before taking his
life, like the executioner of Mary Queen of Scots ;
but this ceremony is now omitted.

The reindeer which were skilfully lassoed and
driven for our benefit are picturesque animals,
with their pale, gray skins and great branching antlers ; the least exacting of all the servitors of man,
as they require no sustenance but the mountain
moss, which they scent even several feet beneath

LAPP WOMAN AND BABY.

the snow.   As the herd ran past, a peculiar crackle of their hoofs—or, as others say, of the knee-joint —was very noticeable, like a quick succession of electric snaps.

We were told that the family relations of the Lapps are very kindly, and that they are a happy, contented race, though inferior to their neighbors, the Finns, in mind and appearance.   I noticed that one ot them who was fishing near our steamer was not allowed to come on board to receive a proffered gratuity from a passenger.   It was handed him from the gangway, no doubt from aversion to closer contact.   So much for our narrow prejudice in favor of soap and water !   On the whole, our visit to the Lapps was one of the most interesting incidents of the voyage, and we came away with considerable respect for a people who, imprisoned two thirds of the year in darkness and storm, and browbeaten by desolate mountains, preserve the graces of contentment and good-nature.

# CHAPTER VII.

IT would be wearisome to my readers to trace too accurately our course around the countless islands, fiords, promontories, and cliffs ; nor would I trench on the provinces of the guidebooks. Now on the right, now on the left, the rapid variety appealed to our attention, and gave no time for reading or for the diversions of an ordinary sea-voyage. Sleep seemed almost culpable during that single day of one hundred and eighty hours, from the midnight of our leaving Trondhjem to the noon of our return ; watches were the relics of a past and fettered existence, "Goodnight" an irony. We had no nights in Norway : the boldest pretension to the name was a gloaming quickly followed by sunrise. We never lighted a candle, and moon and stars were invisible and superfluous. Philosophers say we can do very well without essentials : *"Le luxe c'est la chose bien nécessaire."* We did very well without moon and stars, and the absence of darkness was perpetual pleasure. An astronomer has lately asserted that Io, the satellite of Jupiter nearest that planet, must be far in advance, physically and mentally, of all other bodies in our solar system, inasmuch as it is always bathed in his light, and also in that of his other satellites. And thus during the few weeks in which the inclination of the earth's axis brings these northern regions immediately under solar influence, all vegetable and doubtless all animal life receives increased vitality, which on the coast of Norway is heightened by the invigorating air of ocean. Grass is cut at Hammerfest one month after the snow has melted from the ground.

The midnight spectacle between Tromsöe and Hammerfest was less brilliant than the night before. The atmosphere was cooler, the sky gray and misty; but the veil parted at the critical moment, and, as we had now reached a higher latitude, the sun sank only to a point several degrees above the horizon, before rising again. The interest of this phenomenon is increased by the fact that a clear sky is by no means guaranteed. During the five nights of the voyage within the Arctic Circle it often happens that fogs and rain are incessant. The tourist ship that started June 20th, three days before the *Capella*, never had a glimpse of the sun at midnight during the entire voyage; nor did the one that sailed June 27th. We were therefore unusually favored in seeing it three times in full glory. Of course this is only one episode in the voyage; the marvellous coast scenery is enough in itself to entrance a lover of nature, who readily sees how the mythopœic sense of the early Scandinavians peopled it with deities stern as its snow-clad crags, remorseless as its glaciers, wild and tragic as its winter winds.

We arrived Sunday, the morning of the 27th, at Hammerfest, an unimaginably quaint place and the most northerly town in the world, although tiny settlements have tentatively crept still nearer to the mystic Pole.   The wayward streets straggle around the harbor, which is crowded with unfamiliar craft manned by Danish, Norse, and Russian sailors, brawny and sometimes picturesque, lolling on piles of lumber on shore, pipe in mouth, or taking on cargo.   The nature of the cargo reveals itself—the ubiquitous Cod is master of the field; he is manufactured into oil, he hangs on lines along the harbor, is packed in tumuli on the shore, and is a Smell forever, near and from afar.   We enjoyed the "freedom of the city" for only an hour or so, as our captain had to keep his appointment with the Royal Orb

HAMMERFEST.

at the North Cape twelve hours later. We sent telegrams and letters for the sake of the post-marks; and we looked at the granite meridian column erected to commemorate the measure-ment of the number of degrees between the mouth of the Danube and Hammerfest. The sidewalks are raised two to four feet above the streets, and are reached by rude wooden steps. Several small shops displayed bear-skins, walrus-tusks, and Lapp costumes, and we encountered several Lapps and Finns strolling about in Sunday garb, cleaner and brighter in color, some of them on their way to the church, where the bishop was holding a special service.

We ascended the hill on which the primitive edifice stands, and entering, took places near the door. Two or three hundred decent folk, con-spicuous among them the Lapps, were devoutly listening to a depressing hymn which was followed by a high-keyed, monotonous prayer or exhortation, we could not decide which. Our moments were few; we turned to retreat, but lo! the verger had locked the door inside and put the key in his pocket. We motioned for release, but he shook his head. We waited five impatient minutes, and I then made a second appeal, whispering the word "Dampskib," and pointing on my watch to the hour of its departure. That immovable custodian only shook his head more obstinately, and gazed fixedly at the preacher. We heard the ship's bell ring for the passengers' return, and trembled at the thought of being abandoned to our fate. At last the prayer reached its ultimate note, the key was deliberately turned in the door, we flew to the boat, the boat flew to the steamer, and "home, sweet home" was never more welcome.

# CHAPTER VIII.

AFTER we left Hammerfest and its amenities, the scenery changes in character; Alpine peaks give place to monotonous high plateaux almost bare of vegetation. No sound breaks the silence. No object invades the solitude except flocks of sea-birds which hover over shoals of fish or congregate upon their rocky homes. As the day moves on we watch the sky with deep interest, for filmy fronds and plumes of cloud lightly gather over the blue, and we know that fog and mist will be fatal to our hope for that supreme epoch, our only midnight hour at the North Cape.

"Captain, what of the barometer?"

"'The glass goes up," he replies, not without a deprecating glance around the horizon. He identifies himself with our desires and feels an almost personal responsibility for their fulfilment. We study the heavens like astronomers ; we walk the deck with restless steps, and note all signs. The horizon has grown broader as we advance in latitude, and now, at nearly 72°, its sweep appears illimitable. At eleven o'clock the clouds have all melted out of sight, and a vast unbroken dome of pale blue spreads over a pale lavender sea. We are now passing the island of Mageröe, whose dark slate-rocks are furrowed with deep clefts, and at the extremity rises before us, one thousand feet almost perpendicularly from the water, the isolated

"huge and haggard shape
Of that unknown North Cape."

It is well known now to pilgrims from all touristdom who scramble up the steep, rough path,

drink champagne at the summit, and hide in
hilarity their sentiment or their lack of sentiment
as the case may be.   It is a wearisome climb of at
least an hour, impeded also by loose falling stones,
but is guarded at certain points by ropes, and
this year has been otherwise improved.   A fisherman has built a hut at the base of the rock, where
he lives during the six weeks' summer.   In the
course of another decade or two, no doubt, some
"enterprising" landlord would erect on the top a
" Grand Hôtel du Nord Cap," had not Nature abso-
lutely insisted on all rights of fief and investiture.

The boats were lowered, the passengers then
landed and accompanied by sailors and officers
toiled to the plateau above.   Two or three who
were not strong enough for this task returned to
the steamer with handfuls of wild-flowers, and
contented themselves with the sufficiently extensive
prospect from the captain's bridge.

For myself, I much preferred that quiet post of

observation to the gay champagne-party on the summit. Standing there almost alone, with the silent helmsman at the unmoving wheel, and one or two spell-bound spectators, the poetry of the scene was irresistible. The sun, ten and a half degrees above the northern horizon, with no pomp or panoply of cloud about him, cast a dazzling sheen over the smooth, reflecting waves. Fountains of spray from disporting whales glistened against the pale primrose sky. A single snowy bird skimmed over the surface, its wings tipped with gold as it flew beyond the sight. Far behind us were the dreary islands untenanted by humanity, all Europe and Asia, the emotions and pursuits of busy life, receding into shadowy indistinctness; in front lay the immeasurable sea, quivering in light till lost in indefinite distance. The stillness was almost appalling; not even a ripple broke upon our anchored ship. The light upon sky and water was not the light of day, nor yet of

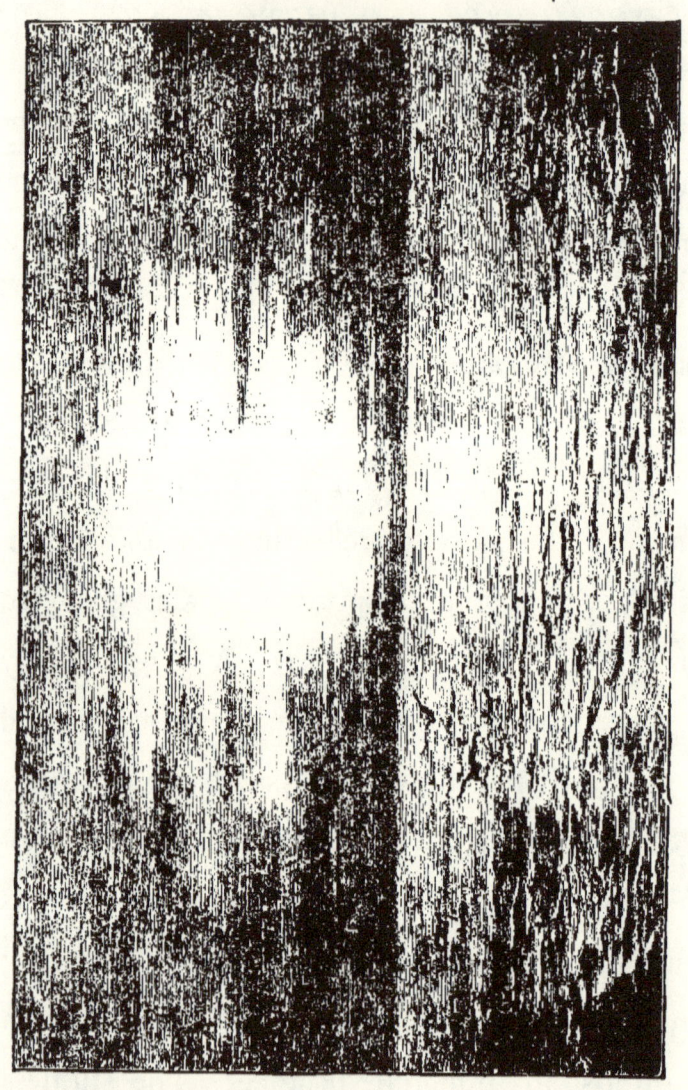

MIDNIGHT SUN—NORTH CAPE.

night, but an ineffably tender blending of both in some divine alembic. As in dreams we are sometimes freed from the fetters of gravitation and soar upward by mere act of volition, so it seemed that from our poise upon that plank it would be easy to rise and float away to the very heart of that heaven where there is no alternation of twilight and dawn, no strophe and antistrophe of light and darkness, because *"there is no night there!"*

Suddenly the boom of a gun announces that the sun has that instant touched his lowest perigee; and with the precision of a royal planet, without Haste and without Rest, he turns his chariot-wheels, flings aside the Yesterday, and inaugurates To-day. Of all the impressive natural spectacles it has been my good fortune to behold, not one has so forcibly appealed to the imagination or has left such vivid trace on memory; and I confess to deep regret when the prow of the ship

turned away from that mysterious, illimitable sea
which seems to whisper

" That which you lose you see around you lying ;
That which you own is far-off and undying."

Our party returned from their scramble up
and down the Cape, wet, tired, and in high spirits,
having dreamed no dreams, save of white bears,
of icebergs, and of all the bristling ramparts from
which the Polar Sea defies science and curiosity.
Let us hope that this one secret may remain a
secret — "One, by Itself, singly, everlastingly
*Alone !*"—lest man should sit down and weep that
not another inch is left for him to conquer.

We nearly missed a tragedy that day. Among
our passengers was a very young Englishman,
who became a conspicuous numeral on our eight-
day clock, partly on account of his irrepressi-
ble high spirits and partly because he was accompanied by a delightful little dog, Puck, in black

and tan. They were both ubiquitous, all over the deck at the same moment, always in a frolic, and *bons camarades* with every one. The master, with a boy's passion for adventure, started to ascend the Cape a little in advance of the party, but, instead of taking the usual safe path, he attempted to climb over a dangerous mass of ice and snow which entirely covered one side of the mountain. The sailors who rowed the boat over protested in vain ; up he went, floundering in snow, until about half-way he sank into a crevasse of ice that left only his head and shoulders visible. A fisherman shouted to the captain, who was in a small boat below. Angry and alarmed, he exclaimed, "He never can climb up, and he cannot get down ;" hurried orders were issued to the sailors, two of whom were dispatched to the rescue from below, and a third, by the usual path; to lower ropes from above. With some difficulty he was hoisted up, white and nearly frozen ; brandy-

flasks were offered by the excited spectators, as
well as sundry disapproving remarks to the reckless
boy, which received no reply except " I must have
looked jolly comical stuck in that icehole!" He
was too plucky to admit that he was half dead with
exhaustion ; but as soon as the midnight coffee
was swallowed he and his faithful dog disappeared
to the cabin for many hours. When there was
a general promenade over a glacier, the following
day, the officer in attendance ordered two sailors
to follow that young man and not lose sight of
him for a moment. By the laws of the steamer
company the captain is required to wait two days
for a passenger detained by casualty ; but this is
an inconvenience to be avoided if possible.

# CHAPTER IX.

THE first day of our return we paused at Swer-
hölt, in the Porsanger fiord, the largest of
several islands monopolized by sea-birds. Up to
the height of several hundred feet it was covered
with thousands of the pretty creatures, that gyrated
with incessant chatter or sat in long, unbroken
lines which resembled rows of pearls on the dark
slate-ledges. At the firing of two or three large
guns they rose in fright and anger, dashed in mad
circles, darted in aimless directions with multi-
plied screams which, made confluent by distance,
resembled, as we sailed away, the distant shriek of
a locomotive : a large number, however, bravely

remained on their nests, but doubtless said all the unpleasant things about us they could think of.

The sea-birds of Norway are so interesting that I would gladly speak of their characters and habits at length, were it not that the monopolists in the "Diffusion of Useful Knowledge" have carried off the entire harvest in this field, without leaving a grain for the modest gleaner. But, even at the risk of telling an oft-told tale, I must repeat what I heard orally about the eider-ducks. These particularly pleasing birds are very numerous in certain localities, and swim fearlessly in the very track of the steamers. When a duck and her mate have flaunted about sufficiently in their honeymoon, and have decided to rear a family and have a "settled home," they waddle to the shore and choose with much fastidiousness, but little perspicuity, an eligible site—generally on the ground in a retreat far from the madding crowd, but occasionally in the cleft of a rock, and they have been

known to take possession of a kitchen-oven. The
nest is made of sea-moss, profusely padded with
tender gray down from the duck's breast. This
accomplished and the eggs laid, the *père de famille*
wanders back to his piscatorial and other amusements in very human style, while the poor
mother finds her nest suddenly stripped of both
eggs and down by the monster, man. She then
makes her way through the waters to her lord,
who has been considerate enough to leave his
address, and they wade back to shore for a second
experiment. But as the duck has already sacri-
ficed her down, the drake now contributes his
own, which, however, is white and less fine and
valuable. The nests are despoiled a second time ;
but if the robbery is again repeated, the discour-
aged birds depart permanently from that part of
the coast. Strangers are not allowed to visit the
bird-islands, and Norwegians are careful to give
the third brood every chance to hatch ; when the

ducklings are large enough to make their first plunge into the sea, they are protected as far as possible from the falcons and other foes which hover above. The islands are sources of large profit, and become heirlooms in families, of sometimes one or two hundred years' descent.

The great white auks which inhabit some of the far northerly islands are models of a social propriety and philanthropy that is limited to Aukland. The females seem to be fewer in number than the males ; and as their conjugal relations are strictly observed, the bachelor-bird is forced to bide his time until death comes to the rescue and gives him an opportunity to unite himself with his brother's widow, which, not being a citizen of England, he can do with impunity. While awaiting this auspicious event, he does not sulk or rush into ornithological dissipation, but makes himself useful by assisting in the care of the young brood, and instructing them in all the rudiments of auk education. (As a plain matter of fact, it might be termed *aukwardness.*) If both parents die, he adopts the entire family!

One day two great eagles flew near the *Capella*, quite formidable enough to justify the stories of their audacity in attacking oxen and other large animals : by the device of dipping their wings in the waves, then in the sand, they blind their prey by flapping against the eyes, when it loses in pain the power of resistance. The lemming, a rodent larger than the water-rat, is a dreaded devastator of wheat-fields, and, notwithstanding the agency of owls and hawks in destroying them, they were formerly made the subject of solemn exorcism by a *Lemming Litany* in the churches.

In the rocky archipelago off this coast is a most desolate and gruesome island to which a noble Danish lady was once banished for some misconduct, and who perished at last by the upsetting of a boat on her way to church in another almost equally weird locality. It offers as melancholy a *mise-en-scène* as the most sensational novelist could desire.

Again we paused *en route,* to visit an extensive glacier where most of the passengers landed, walked a mile and a half over a marshy plain to the base of the field of ice, which they traversed for a short distance. It was never a *dolce far niente* to make one's rather perilous way over those beautiful blue, slippery and jagged tracts, and one of my party described her experience in this way : "I was flat on my back or down on my knees most of the time, although there was a sailor on each side and an officer in front of me ; the sole of one of my boots was torn off, and I nearly lost the other ; it poured as we returned, and every one was drenched ; I went to bed after a cup of hot ginger-tea, and my clothes went to the engine-room to dry : but, notwithstanding all this, it was the most exhilarating experience of the whole

voyage, full of fun and rivalry for the farthest
point."

The final act in our varied excursion was a visit
to a whale which had been caught the previous
day and was lying on the premises of a factory
near Tromsöe, where they dispose of the mortal
remains of the race—a cetacean crematory which
gives out an odor not to be described. The creature, nearly fifty feet long, lay upon the shore,
and beside it a baby-whale which had never
even begun its briny career. The sight was a
privilege, no doubt; but not one to linger over,
for already the workmen were hewing at one massive longitudinal half; the other, still unmutilated,
was by request turned over for exhibition—and all
Arabia's spices and Lubin's perfumes would have
been overpowered by the odor that pervaded the
place. A friendly warning beforehand had led me
to bring a bottle of eau-de-Cologne, with which
we nearly suffocated ourselves to no purpose.

The genial festivities of the "last dinner" on board ship have generally lost prestige since the ranks of travel have enlarged ; but the parting banquet on the *Capella* was a pleasant reminiscence quite in keeping with the voyage.   Marvels of confectionery decorated the tables, as well as all the varieties of fish, flesh, and fowl which Norway offers at this season.   Our neighbors the Russian General, the Upsala Professor, and the Swedish Member of Parliament had previously held a conclave, the result of which was a complimentary flow of champagne, and a long, solemn oration, in French, from the M. P., in which our voyage was compared to the passage of the Israelites over the Red Sea, conducted by the captain in the *rôle* of Moses !   If this speech was a fair specimen of those offered to the Swedish Parliament, that august body is to be pitied.   The captain replied in a few modest and hearty words, and a round of toasts in three or four languages, ending in the old Scandinavian "*Skaal!*" which to English ears is more suggestive of death than of festivity. Then followed compliments to the "orator of the day," the ship, and the officers; and when we all went on deck to sip our *café noir*, and to watch the waning and waxing of our last nocturne in northern waters, a final resolution was proposed, namely, "Never, never to sail on any ocean but the Arctic, or in any ship but the *Capella*, Iveson, master."

Our tour ended practically when we landed at Trondhjem; and it was not without a tinge of regret that we obeyed the imperious mandate of the locomotive, and found ourselves, after one night's ride through charming scenery, at Christiania, *en route* for Sweden.

We were leaving much unseen, especially Bergen, quaintest of the three cities; the eminently picturesque fiords in its vicinity, and the very primitive Telemarken district on the post-road thence to Christiania. Pleasures, however, must be economized, not exhausted : enough—for the moment—of Norway summer nights ; but their unique and tender beauty will rest on our memories with the vivid hues of an after-glow on snow-crowned mountain-heights.

# CHAPTER X.

*(Par Parenthèse.)*

SWEDEN is to most travellers a parenthesis between Norway and Russia, comprised of Stockholm and the Dalsland and Götha canals. The latter form so pleasing a feature that it is certainly unwise to fly by rail to the capital without allowing an added thirty hours for the sake of seeing these celebrated water-routes which are justly the pride of the country. We left Christiania by rail at 7 A.M., had a fine view of the city, its hills and fiord, on starting, and after six or seven hours through a fertile and pretty but not impressive region we arrived at Ed, whence five minutes on a local train brought us to the waiting steamer on the Dalsland Canal—a Lilliputian craft only sixteen feet broad, clean and comfortable enough for our voyage, if such it may be called, of twenty-four hours. We were the only passengers, except an occasional peasant or two on and off, and the captain, who spoke tolerable English, was assiduous in his efforts to entertain and instruct us; and so, as the sleepy little steamer puffed gently through the water, we subsided into a lotus-eating dream of canal gliding into lake, and lake into canal, of pauses at the numerous locks, descent between ponderous stone walls, and then a rush of waters and we were off again—always past wooded shores overhanging trees, lovely islands, and as unlike as possible most canals, except some of those in Holland. The Dalsland unites several beautiful lakes between Lake Wenner and Norway, and as they rise to different heights, making the sum total about three hundred feet, the locks are many. We often walked

from one to another, gathered scant raspberries,
wild roses galore, lilies of the valley, the flower of
Baldur the Beautiful, and pale little pansies which
in Scandinavian legends are called the Devil's
flowers, as the magpie is still the Devil's bird.

Everything that lives, plant or animal, was endowed by those old Goths, even more than by the
Greeks, with moral attributes, good or evil. It
was only by an arrow made from the mistletoe,
which has no individual existence, that Baldur
was killed by his enemy Asgaard, all things that
grow and live having sworn to the goddess Freya
that they would not lend themselves to the purpose.

Our steamer, for some inscrutable reason,
stopped during the night at a place called Bil-
lingsfors, where passengers are furnished with beds
on shore when the resources of the boat are
exhausted. It boasts only four cabins, with one
bed in each—a penitential pallet, as unrelenting
as that of a Camaldoli monk. The finest point

on the route is at Hafverud, where, owing to
some local difficulty of rock and soil, an aque-
duct was constructed over which the boat passes,
presenting a unique spectacle from the shore below. Although this canal is well worth seeing,
it must be admitted that its scenery is tame and
monotonous after the fiords and mountain-ranges
of Norway. It were better if possible to visit
Sweden first. We left the steamer at Köpmanna-
bro, where we took the rail to Trollhatten, occupy-
ing two to three hours.

At the hotel restaurant here we ate our first
Swedish dinner, somewhat unique in appointment at the railway stations and ordinary inns.
The table was nearly covered with from a dozen
to twenty "appetizers," or small dishes of as
many varieties of salt and smoked fish, sausages,
and pickled vegetables, amid which brandy and
liqueurs were conspicuous. The hot dishes were
on another table, from which we helped ourselves;

and when we paid the account, we made our own
statement of the items, the correctness of which
was unquestioned. The fruit of the season was
wild mountain strawberries, which were abundant
and good.

Half an hour's drive took us to Trollhatten
Falls, which are considered even finer than those
at Schaffhausen, and on our way we stopped to
see the remarkable locks of the Götha Canal, a
great triumph of engineering skill when they were
cut, but probably surpassed by the science of our
day. It was early in the fifteenth century that the
problem was first presented of uniting the east and
west coasts through the numerous intervening
lakes and rivers, and thus making an island of the
southern part of Sweden. The cataracts and
rocks proved too formidable for the engineers of
that period. Several subsequent attempts were
made, which served the purpose tolerably well,
but the *fait accompli* was due to Ericsson, who

TROLLHATTEN FALLS.

added several new and larger locks for the transport of vessels from the North Sea to Lake Wenner by a watery staircase one hundred and forty-four feet above the sea. The locks, which are cut through solid rock and overshadowed by trees, are as picturesque as practical.

The Falls of Trollhatten far surpass in breadth all cataracts to be seen in Norway, as they are an outlet from one of the largest lakes in Europe; they are six in number within a hundred and fifty yards, and the effect is of force rather than of grandeur, as the enormous volume of water is thwarted and fretted by great masses of rocks and islands in the middle of the stream. In fact they form a terrific whirl and roar of speed, which tosses its white foam high in air and deserves all the adjectives that describe "how the water comes down from Lodore," until they subside into a flow of crested rapids. A fine abiding-place was this for all that fanciful race of wood and

water spirits who were as capricious as the elements which they personated—the Grims, spirits
of the cataracts ; the Haafmen, people of the sea ;
the Strömkarls, deities of the rivers.

The old Swedes are said to have been even more
fanciful than the Norwegians : one of the most
poetic ideas was that elves and trees were identi-
cal—trees by day, elves by night ; when enemies
invaded their territory, battalions of birch and
aspens marched out in solid phalanx to attack
them, but with the dawn of day marched back
again and resumed their vegetable immobility.
That these superstitions were actual motors in
their lives is proved by the fact that in the state
papers of Sweden records still exist of trials and
condemnations of men and women for witchcraft,
more legalized than the spasmodic crusades against
Anglo-Saxon witches at about the same period.
One of the many legends that cluster around
Trollhatten Falls is that of a young girl who was

imprisoned in a neighboring cavern inhabited by brigands, and threatened with some awful death if she revealed their hiding-place or attempted to escape. On a Christmas night, when the ground was white with snow, she obtained leave to go out for a bundle of straw, which she dropped blade by blade on her return, and thus disclosed the secret of the cavern, and led to the capture and execution of the robbers.

The custom of putting bells on cows doubtless originated in Scandinavia, where they were first employed as a defence against the Trolls, or spirits of the woods, who were believed to milk the animals at night unless warned away by the tintinnabulation.

The train from Gotheburg took us on at 8 P.M., and after fourteen hours of that passive exercise which goes by the name of sleep in a railway-carriage we found ourselves delightfully comfortable in the Grand Hotel at Stockholm. Breakfast was as

welcome as were our luxurious rooms, for the restaurant on the road afforded nothing but bread
and the cruelty of "appetizers," which create a
want without supplying it. Travel certainly owes
many of its pleasures to contrast. We were
charmed with even the first appearance of Stockholm. It is certainly the most picturesquely situated of all European cities, as it is built on several
islands in Lake Mälar, and also has a harbor on
an arm of the Baltic. In these bright waters ply
active little steamers, large vessels produce-laden,
white-winged skiffs, and tiny row-boats, in endless
number and variety. Handsome bridges, many
broad, regular streets, substantial buildings, and,
dominating almost every part of the city, the dignified royal palace, complete the picture. The
"Venice of the North," as of course it is dubbed,
bears not the slightest resemblance to the Venice
of the South, except that they are both built on
islands connected by bridges. The style of archi-

tecture, the aspect of the people, the atmosphere, and the fashion of the water-craft are far as the antipodes asunder.

SWEDISH PEASANT AND BABY.

We passed a week at Stockholm with great enjoyment, heightened by the arrival of friendly companions of *Capella* memory, and we could have lingered a month or two without weariness; for, after due attention to whatever is characteristic and historical, there is endless amusement in steamer excursions, to charming suburbs and gay, handsome gardens echoing with good music. It is, in fact, the only enjoyable summer city in Europe, and the air is irreproachable. The mediæval castle of Gripsholm is not far off, filled with furniture and tapestry that would break the heart of a covetous collector; and a day or two might well be spent at Upsala, the intellectual centre of Sweden, as it once was the stronghold of Scandinavian paganism. Our only regret here, as elsewhere, was the necessity for postponing to the shadowy by-and-by many such temptations.

On one of those small, neat steamers that ply to and from the island of Drottningholm we met, one day, a distinguished gentleman whose courteous attentions during our stay in Stockholm gave us much information and enjoyment—one of those happily-attuned mortals whose wealth of facts and fancies finds equally facile expression in a dozen different languages. He pioneered us through the mazes of the park, which is a modest copy of Versailles adorned with sculptures in marble and bronze, to a Chinese toy of a palace, built and furnished throughout with Celestial handicraft as a surprise to a royal lady on her birthday. Adjoining this is a small building called the dining-room, where some sovereign of mechanical turn constructed a table that slides through the floor, and is served with successive courses without apparent agency. The large palace of Drottningholm, which is an occasional residence, contains the usual fine furniture, porcelain, and pictures, under watch and ward of uncommonly civil custodians. The principal attraction is a ball-room surrounded on all sides by a distinguished corps of Swedish and foreign monarchs in their respective uniforms.

The excursion to Drottningholm is very charming
on a summer evening, when a film of gold is spread
over verdant shores, white villas embowered in silvery birches, flying boats, and calm blue waters.
On our return our friend proposed the ascent of an
immense elevator, whence the whole map—of city,
islands, Lake Mälar and the Baltic—photographed
itself on memory.  It was a generous convulsion
of nature that bestowed upon this sheet of water
more than twelve hundred islands, in every stage
of fertility from barren rocks and primeval forests
to high cultivation.

The royal palace, an unusually dignified and
massive structure, stands on a rocky eminence, and
commands fine views of sea and land.  Of course
we paid the usual visit to the interior ; but as state
apartments repeat themselves in all royal resi-
dences (outside of Russia), when a tourist has
promenaded over a few hundred polished floors
and has glanced at several thousand gilded chairs,

mosaic tables, porcelain vases, and the like, under
the vigilant eyes of polyglot ciceroni, he is ready
to register a vow of disdainful and eternal import,
which if broken must at least be unrecorded in
the breach. Therefore I limit all description of
the Stockholm palace to the private apartments of
the family, which are worth noting because they
are as unpretentious and homelike as those of
any private citizen, graced, as usual, by the refine-
ments of books, photographs, paintings, hand-
worked cushions, and various pretty but inexpen-
sive knick-knacks. To the very simple apartment
of one of the princes is attached his work-room,
which contains several pieces of mechanism from
his own hand. On this side of the Muscovite
frontier the divinity that doth hedge a king clips
its foliage every decade more nearly to the popular
level.

The National Museum is a handsome edifice
with a portal of green marble, surmounted by

medallion portraits of Swedish artists. Colossal
marble statues of Odin, Thor, and Baldur guard
the vestibule ; outside is a highly-commended
group in bronze of two combatants in a "girdle-
duel"—a *tour de force* of sculpture which might
better have spent itself on a less ghastly subject.
The principal attraction of the museum is the extremely rich ethnographical collection, which be-
gins at prehistoric flint and bronze periods. The
native gold ornaments of the Runic age are particularly tasteful, and often refined in decoration.
Very interesting also are the implements and furniture of the three past centuries, arranged together according to their respective dates. The
gallery of antique and modern sculpture boasts of
one antique treasure in the "Sleeping Endymion,"
a life-size statue which was found in Adrian's villa
and purchased by the art-loving king, Gustavus III.

The sculptors of Sweden take higher rank than
its painters, but it is to be regretted that they

should not perpetuate the weird grandeur of
Scandinavian heroes and deities instead of feebly
repeating the classic and worn-out gods and god-
desses of the Mediterranean. A nude Venus and
a vine-wreathed Bacchus on the shores of the
Baltic are as incongruous with the climate and
traditions of their present habitat as the obelisk of
Rameses on the banks of the Hudson.

The room dedicated to Dutch and Flemish
painters presents many admirable specimens of
Rembrandt, Van Dyck, Teniers, and others; but
on the whole this art-treasury is rather mediocre,
especially in the Italian department. The modern
Scandinavian collection offers more of interest;
but as the artists study principally in German
schools, they have no distinctive national style.

There is one large canvas on which Tiderman
represents one of those fanatical preachers often
found in Norway who portray the "terrors of the
law" with the impassioned fury of the old Puri-

tans, and with the same effect on the audience; women fall fainting to the floor, and even men are spell-bound with fear. The picture is highly realistic in variety of feature and expression. More attractive, however, are the cottage-interiors and portraits of the Swedish artist Amalia Lindegren, whose peasant-children have the grace and innocence of Arcadia under their homely garb.

The shops of Stockholm are not beguiling; old silver at "Hammei's," Dalecarlian costumes and excellent colored photographs of peasants, were our only temptations. Theatres were closed for the summer; but there was good music in open-air concerts, especially at the Djärgarden, an extensive park reached either by boat or train, where orderly crowds flock every pleasant evening; and we have memories of a gay little dinner there with tourist friends in the veranda of the restaurant, with echoes of Wagner and Strauss in the evening air, sunshine gilding the trees, rippling

laughter, and of course the all-enveloping blue in-
cense and aroma of the "plant divine, of rarest
virtue."

It is superfluous to say that the Swedes have
a national reputation for courtesy and hospitality, as well as for the sterling virtues of the Norwegians. We could not ex-
pect, in a mere *vol d'oiseau*
between two seas, to have any
personal experience of this
agreeable fact ; but in streets
and shops their politeness of
manner was noticeable. They
are a better - looking people

SWEDISH COSTUME.

than their neighbors on either side, though fair hair
and serene blue eyes are not universal ornaments.

We saw many Dalecarlian women in the streets
in their becoming costume, which consists of
full white sleeves, colored bodice fastened with
silver or gilded chains and profuse ornaments,

short dark skirts, a high, close-fitting woollen cap, and red stockings. They are conservative in dress, like the people of the Telemarken province of Norway, hard workers, and don their costumes as every-day clothing, not merely to pose in like the Tyrolese and Romans. In the Moosebacke quarter, the "Moses Hill," stands the picturesque red-brick church of the Riddaesholm with its tall perforated iron spire—a Walhalla of fame where repose in melancholy state kings and nobles of the Seraphim order. Its bell, called the Seraphim, never rings, nor are services performed, except for a funeral pageant. Innumerable flags of various countries and colors droop from monuments and armorial bearings which line the interior walls, in the conventional style that must continue until, in the development of higher faith, men devise some more cheerful form of commemoration.

When our bright and busy week in Stockholm had reached its close, we all felt that Fate might do something much more displeasing than to send us back some future day to that charming summer city. We said farewell over the "beaker's brim" to our courteous Swedish friend, and, with passports *"viséd"* by the Russian consul, embarked on the steamer *Constantin* for the land of the Tsar.

# CHAPTER XI.

*(An Episode.)*

AS we steamed, about 6 o'clock P.M., out of the harbor where sits on her throne of islands the Queen of the Baltic, the fair city presented a lovely picture: spires, roofs, and the conspicuous royal palace gleamed in gold; white suburban villas made points of light in wooded headlands; broad masses of trees formed contrasting shadows; half-furled sails and tall masts sentinelled the shining waters. Floating onwards, the glittering details gradually concentrated into a point of unity which soon was lost to sight on the misty horizon. A few hours later the sun also quenched his fires in the sea, but left a promise

for the morrow in those silvery gradations of neb-
ulous light which in northern skies intervene between his parting and his return. The Baltic,
like the Mediterranean, has no tides, is neither
very deep nor very salt, and, though capable of
being roused to passion, is a better disposed ocean
than some of its neighbors.

With the exception of a few hours in open sea
the first night, our picturesque and tortuous
track ran between an archipelago of islands on
the Finnish coast, many of which are bare red-
granite rocks or heaps of stones abraded by un-
ceasing waves. The voyage to St. Petersburg
occupies three nights, the intervening days being
pleasantly diversified by halts at Abo, the old capital of Finland, and at Helsingfors, the new capital. The *Constantin* is one of the best steamers
on the Swedish line ; the cabins are comfortable,
—and with twenty-one different "appetizers" at
every meal, what more could be desired ?

Our trio had now enlarged itself to a quartet,
and gained the only element it lacked by the ad-
dition of a young American, whose personal
characteristics and previous acquaintance with St.
Petersburg completed the measure of our enjoyment.   Ladies can travel alone through the high-
ways of Russia with safety and comfort, but the
"right sort of man" is undeniably an acquisition.
Our *preux chevalier* was the right sort of man.
The passengers were all Swedes, Finns, and Russians—among the latter a lady, who was so con-
genial, as well so kindly helpful to us in St. Petersburg, that our accidental acquaintance has passed
into friendly permanence.

We arrived at Abo (pronounced Obo) the
morning after leaving Stockholm.   An ancient cathedral and a more ancient castle, both of some
historical interest, stand prominently on the harbor ; and on a high hill in the town is an obser-
vatory well known to scientists.

Finland has always occupied the undesirable position of a small country between two large ones, tossed like a ball back and forth, until it finally was grasped by the talons of the double-headed eagle, where it remains, under the title of Grand Duchy. It retains its religious and constitutional privileges—under bit and bridle, however, of imperial representatives. It is a watery domain brimming over with fiords, lakes, and swamps, even its name being derived from *fen*, or morass. With grasping neighbors on either side, pestilence, fires, and famine at various periods, and deadly quarrels among its early tribes, it has had from the beginning a hard struggle for existence. Since the transferrence of the capital to Helsingfors Åbo is a deserted village : a few vessels lie idly in the harbor ; one or two small hotels wait idly on the quay. In the broad, silent streets, the houses, built of wood, are only one story high and very far apart, their doorways level with the ground.

There is only one thing to be seen—the uncouth Gothic cathedral ; and unless one is in a mood for horrors it may better be avoided, for in the crypt the dead stand dressed in the garb of the living, as they do in the ghastly church of the Capucines at Rome and the cemetery at Palermo.

By the captain's advice we decided on a drive to the park of Runsala, four or five miles away, which would at least take us to fresh fields and pastures new. The national "droschkies" are small, narrow, dingy one-horse vehicles which possess unlimited capacity for jolt and rattle ; are started at full gallop, and continued at as breathless a pace as if pursued by a pack of wolves. Remonstrance was hopeless, for the drivers talked Finnish, and we did not ; and moreover it is the national pace. However, the park was reached without accident ; and though it has no merit of cultivation, it affords pretty views and shaded walks. The restaurant dinner served on the veranda was rather eccentric in quality and condiment ; but on the whole this excursion is more entertaining than to sit idly on the deck while the steamer pauses in the harbor.

Helsingfors, where we stopped the following day, has been a vampire to Åbo and sucked its very life-blood—the university, the population, the seat of government. The approach is very imposing from the sea, for it is guarded by the fortress of Sveaborg, which extends over seven islands ; on the shore opposite stands a large and handsome Russian cathedral with conspicuous white dome and gilded spire. The streets are broad, with much parade of pompous architecture of no distinctive character, relieved by avenues of trees and pleasant walks. As we had seven or eight hours to while away on shore, we first turned our steps to the crowded market in an open square, where a motley crowd, roughly clothed, bought and sold such quantities of meat and fish as precluded all

ideas of famine in the land, apart from the cart-
loads of coarse black bread which looked less
like the staff of life than its cudgel.

We had sometimes wished we might find some
locality not yet penetrated by the ubiquitous
*"articles de fantaisie"* of Paris—and we did find
it in Norway; but here in Finland it was a tire-
some reminder of the ever-decreasing size of this
petty planet to be offered by a peasant-woman in
the market little bottles of Atkinson's perfumes !
And then we said, "There will be no escape
from 'high civilization' until we go to the fair at
Nijni Novgorod." After a walk to the cathedral,
and much admiration of the fine paintings in its
gilded Ikonostas, we drove to the very pretty Bruns-
park, a gay summer resort with the usual accompaniments of restaurant, music, and open-air
theatre. Our dinner was supplemented by profuse
and delicious strawberries, and we wandered under
the trees until it was time to return to the steamer.

Then we conned till a late hour our Russian phrase-book, and mounted the numeral pyramid from "oden" to " dvàtzat," " tritsat," " sòrok," and " sto," under the spur of to-morrow's requirements. The numbers and a few phrases are essential in Russia, as elsewhere, unless one is willing to be buttoned every instant to a *valet de place.*

Even the guide-books fail to invest Finland with sparkling interest, archæological or historic ; one infers that, like Fingal's cave and many other places, it may be worth seeing, but is not worth going to see, as all its characteristics, moral and material, are either semi-Swedish or semi-Russ. It finds favor with sporting fishermen, and its cataracts and most of its lakes tempt artists, though its trees are stunted and the atmosphere is generally cold and dull. However, as a geographical lesson the southern shore breaks very pleasantly the summer *traversée* to St. Petersburg.

# RUSSIAN DAYS.

RUSSIAN CHURCH.

# RUSSIAN DAYS.

## CHAPTER I.

### ST. PETERSBURG.

DURING the past few years so many lorg-
nons and field-glasses have been levelled at
Russia with curiosity and criticism ; so many
native and foreign writers have dramatically pictured its past, present, and prospective story, that
the entire country is now supposed to stand under
the blaze of electric light, with two important ex-
ceptions—the plans of the Nihilists and the pro-
jects of the Czar. Our innocent Russian days
were quite undisturbed by these problems : we
merely glanced over the glittering surface like

birds briefly perched on a telegraph-wire ; we were thorough optimists, and entered into all the novelties of sight and sound with hearty satisfaction. Therefore I do not pretend to add another canvas to the already crowded gallery ; I merely trace an outline and throw in a few dashes of "local color."

The approach to St. Petersburg on a fine summer morning owes its exceptional attraction to art rather than to nature. There are no rugged shore-rocks resonant to the sea ; no mountains in the distance ; no verdant hills to grace the foreground : but the level monotone of earth and sky is broken by many islands and several fortresses on either side, chief of which latter is Cronstadt, with walls of solid granite ten feet thick. It dominates a forest of tall masts of men-of-war bearing flags of every color, but principally of the national black and yellow. Then appear on the smooth-water surface dark contrasting masses of merchant-

ships, of yachts flying before the wind, of heavily
laden steam-tugs ; and as our vessel advances, a
star shines on the horizon which grows in magni-
tude, until it reveals itself as the great gilded
dome of the cathedral of St. Isaac. Gradually
the sky - outline is broken by other burnished
domes, by pale green domes studded with stars
of gold, by glittering crosses and arrows of light,
which compose the tiara of the city of the Tsar.

Yet a little farther onward, and massive granite
quays, stately palaces, countless cupolas, lofty
watch-towers, and monoliths of red granite proudly
pose upon the delta formed by the broad silvery
Neva and its outspread branches. Whether we
will or not, this marvellous city which sprung in
a brief historic day from an almost arctic swamp
compels admiration, as a *tour de force* if nothing
more.

As we landed at the quay of the custom-house,
*moujiks* with long hair and russet beards trans-

ferred our luggage to a crowded platform, where our passports were demanded and our impedimenta very thoroughly scrutinized by civil officers who spoke both French and German. As soon as it was decided that we were innocent of evil intent towards "*la Sainte Russie*," we were conducted to the omnibus of the Hôtel de l'Europe, to which we had written for rooms. We had a long drive through some of the finest parts of the city, and a glimpse of the great square on which stand the palace of the Admiralty, the Winter Palace, St. Isaac's Cathedral, and the colossal bronze statue of Peter the Great, before we turned into the celebrated Nevski Prospekt, and thence came by a few steps to our hotel.

We found excellent quarters in readiness for us ; but the courteous manager, in pursuance of the usual Russian fashion of offering a large choice of rooms, pioneered us over miles of corridors ; for this *Gostinnitza*, like the Hôtel du Louvre in

Paris, covers an enormous space. We decided on the luxurious suite he had assigned us, and settled down to domesticity under the patronage of the saints whose images appear unobtrusively on the walls of every Russian room. Like the gods of ancient Greece, the pictured saints are more numerous than the people ; no cook would remain an hour in a house where there was not one in the kitchen. The servants who attended us, however, were Germans ; and there are at least two English *valets de place*, one of whom, named Alexander, we can especially commend. We expected to find Russian vapor-baths in perfection, but were assured that they are by no means so well appointed as in Paris or New York, at least for ladies.

After our luncheon, in which strawberries, melons, and *tchai slamonum*—tea with thin slices of lemon—pleasantly figured, we started with the eagerness of children for that first general orienta-

tion which defines the chaos of a new city.   We
noticed at once the dress of the coachmen, which

RUSSIAN COACHMAN.

consists of a dark-blue woollen caftan that extends
to the feet; it is plain over the shoulders, and
crosses from right to left with large filigree silver

buttons, and five more on the left side behind ;
the skirt falls in full plaits, especially at the back,
and a belt somewhat like the border of a cashmere
shawl passes round the waist. A flat cloth cap,
larger above than below, and high boots over the
trousers, which are not visible, complete the costume. The drivers hold one rein in each hand,
and guide the horses by the voice rather than the
whip.

The first thing that strikes one in St. Petersburg is the prodigality of space and gigantic
dimensions of the streets, which give to even four-
storied houses an appearance of being built low.
The right angles are as rigid as the squares of a
chess-board ; there are no narrow, crooked lanes
as in other European cities. The pavements are
generally bad, owing to the marshy subsoil ; but
this is less important, because half the year they
are excellently paved with snow. The great or
Bolshaya Neva River passes through the centre,

and with its branch the little or Malaya Neva forms islands, on which other portions are built. Two hundred years ago this river was unknown except to Finnish huntsmen in the untrodden forests through which it flows from Lake Onega to the bay of Finland. It is as broad as the Rhine at Cologne; its clear, blue waters are not only a beautiful feature, but they supply the wants of the city. At the same time they are a perpetual menace, for, though guarded by massive granite embankments, they are only two feet below the level of the streets; and when in the spring the north wind blows a gale, from the narrow part of the bay the waters of the Neva are forced back, and, if the ice happens to be breaking up at the same time, inundations are inevitable. Therefore, when warning guns are heard from the fortress, those who live in cellars and basements look for safe shelter, and sentries in their boxes are provided for. Numerous handsome bridges span

the waters, which are animated by fleets of row-
boats, yachts, and commercial vessels. In winter
these liquid roads are solidly frozen, and sledges
supplant the sails.

Previous to our journey hither many sugges-
tions had been offered that winter is *par excel-
lence* the time to visit this hyperborean capital ;
but the fact is that, like the duplicate shield which
was gold on one side and silver on the other, St.
Petersburg has two totally different aspects.
Most alluring we found it in summer, with its
verdant parks, blue waters, green and golden
domes, and soft, diaphanous nights ; and with
such generosity of space and air that in even the
warmth of July one is not oppressed as in other
cities. We drove up and down the Nevski Prospekt, which corresponds as an artery of fashionable commerce with the Alcala in Madrid, Rue de
Rivoli in Paris, and Regent's Street in London,
but is a *mélange* of shops, palaces, monuments,

and churches far more imposing than either.
The architecture is not distinctive in any part
of the city. Neither Peter the Great nor his
successors could create a new structural art :
they united classic and Renaissance forms with
Byzantine domes and decorations. Critics have
called it a city of architectural shams, and com-
plain that porticos and pillars are of plaster-
covered brick, façades are flat, and balconies
inconsistent with an arctic climate. But, on
the other hand, nowhere else are found such
superb or abundant monoliths as those of the
Finland red granite, which give color and majesty to churches and palaces. The one erected
to Alexander I. near the Winter Palace is considered the greatest of modern times—a single
shaft eighty-four feet high, beautifully polished,
surmounted by a gilded angel bearing a cross ;
the base and pedestal, twenty-five feet high, of the
same material.

The houses are built in apartments which apparently consist of a series of salons, as they are furnished with luxurious couches converted into beds at night. The ladies' dresses are kept folded in the boxes in which they come from Paris, and other accessories of the toilet are removed from sight ; so that the salons are always *en grande tenue,* and the restful privacy of a pretty sleeping-room, so dear to the Anglo-Saxon heart, is an unappreciated luxury.

Many of the shops are painted on the outside with representations of their wares : vividly-colored fruits and vegetables, bunches of grapes and flasks of wine, pianos, ladies' cloaks surmounted by hats, and many other temptations appeal to those who are unable to read. Decidedly, we were of that illiterate class. We had pored over those perplexing letters until we could pronounce the words with tolerable correctness : but it was another thing to translate them.

At first sight the signs suggest an alphabetical cyclone ; but their large ornate characters at a little distance look like a sculptured frieze of gold on ground of red or blue.

It was not the season for parade of equipages, and we saw none that were distinctive. The uncomfortable but convenient little droschkies flew about in swarms, for there are few pedestrians in this city of magnificent distances. Here and there were Cossack soldiers in long blue coats or caftans and high white, red, or blue caps edged with sheepskin, and armed with swords, poniards, pistols, and rifles ; and everywhere moujiks, in red or blue shirts, belted round the waist, extending below the short loose jacket, and loose trousers thrust into big boots. Apropos is a story, *se non vero, ben trovato*, cited in recent journals, of a reply made by Bismarck to Lord Dufferin, who had asked his opinion of the Russian character : "My dear lord, the Russian is a very good

fellow *until he tucks in his shirt"*—a caustic com-
ment quite characteristic of the Premier.

COSSACK OFFICER.

I should put in a deferential protest against his
sweeping criticism: the Russians who diffuse

themselves through various countries have the reputation of being very charming people—vivacious, friendly, hospitable, highly intelligent and accomplished, and some, of my own intimate acquaintance, are as true-hearted and good as the world affords.

### THE SHOPS.

We noticed many little stalls for the sale of pictured saints, holy oil and water ; boxes for sacred offerings at the corners of the streets, on bridges, at the exits of markets; and reverent crossings and prostrations before frequent shrines of prayer. In all this was a touch of the Orient ; but we were not yet beyond the intrusion of French signs and German merchandise. The road that leads beyond these too-familiar objects is far away from St. Petersburg. But we did visit shops which every feminine heart would appreciate ; one of Russian embroidered costumes, towels and table-cloths, and also the exquisitely fine white goat's-wool shawls from Orenburg, made by hand from threads of fairy texture. The finest of these shawls requires the work of two women for two years ; it was more gossamer than the finest thread lace, a mere mist from a summer cloud, and correspondingly fragile. One of the largest size, three yards square, we saw drawn through a finger-ring, and the fair owner intended to wear it at her wedding instead of the conventional tulle or Brussels lace. A similar shawl was presented to Patti on her last visit to Russia, and she wore it over a white-satin tunic. Even the inferior qualities that cost only eight or ten rubles are as soft as down.

Another specialty is the silver-work, which far exceeds in beauty, as well as in weight, that of other countries. The fabric of enamelled gold and silver gilt is beautiful enough to justify a compound fracture of the tenth commandment : it is

covered with the very finest enamel of various colors, principally light blue and ruby, laid on with
twisted threads of gold that would pass through
a needle's eye.    Jewel-caskets,    toilet    articles,
sugar-bowls, spoons, etc., fill one shop exclusive-
ly.   This fine enamel is rather new, and therefore
little known outside of Russia ; but even the older
fabric on silver gilt is also beautiful, though not
quite so delicate.   The best shop is that of Ivan
Petrovitch  Chlebnekoff,   on   the   Nevski   Prospekt.

The   fur-shops   are   ruinously   attractive,  especially the sable, which we had never seen so fine
and dark.   The London merchants declare that
they procure some of the very best qualities ; but
the Moscow dealers assured us that they never sell
those outside of Russia.   Sables are always expensive because so small a portion of the little animal
is of the coveted dark color.   The famous Potemkin had a muff which cost a thousand guineas.

Ordinary furs may be bought more reasonably here than elsewhere.

There are several shops of Circassian embroideries, but we were advised to buy those in Moscow. As there are no Leghorn hats made in Leghorn, and no Venetian blinds in Venice, so there is no Russian leather in Russia; the raw material being exported to Germany, where it is manufactured into the universal pocket-books and portfolios. There is a great two-storied bazaar, the Gostinnoi Dvor, which is stocked with all possible articles for household use and old bric-à-brac shops, but very little that a traveller would desire except the Circassian and Caucasian shawls and sashes, better obtained in Moscow. It is, however, all worth a visit of curiosity.

A few pounds of the best tea is a desirable purchase; for, as it is brought overland through Siberia, the flavor is much more delicate than that which comes by sea. The yellow and the white, made from the first tiny buds of the plant, form a nerve-exciting beverage which should rarely be indulged in. It costs from four or five rubles to fifty a pound (a ruble being generally equivalent to seventy-five cents or three shillings sterling, but in the present state of Russian funds a third less). *Tchai slamonum* is made from an inferior quality of leaf; but we found it very palatable—a harmless beverage, as universal as beer in Germany and *vin ordinaire* in France.

### THE CATHEDRAL.

The world-renowned Cathedral of St. Isaac's stands conspicuously in a large open square, surrounded by several of the finest edifices and monuments in the city. A few words will recall the many descriptions given of it by clever writers. It is a Greek cross in form; the four ends are terminated by porticos which are reached by flights of red-granite steps ; above these stand stately pol-

ished columns of the same material, sixty feet
high and seven in diameter, with bronze Corin-
thian capitals. They support a massive frieze
from which rises the dome of bronze overlaid with
burnished gold, also supported by a circle of granite

THE NEVA—THE BRIDGE—ST. ISAAC'S.

pillars. From the centre, again, rises the rotunda,
or lantern, a miniature repetition of the whole
edifice, surmounted by a golden cross. Four
smaller domes stand above each end of the arms
of the cross and complete the harmony. Each

flight of steps as well as each column is formed of
a single block of granite : all of them, as well as
hundreds more in other churches and palaces, were
conveyed from Finland on rollers, their weight
being too great for wheels.   The Tsars are as
rich as were the Pharaohs in unlimited quarries
of marble.

Ponderous sculptured bronze doors lead to the
interior, where floor, walls, and supporting pillars
are of polished marbles, verde antique, Sienna yellow, porphyry, and jasper.   Gilded angels of various sizes, pictures of Christ, the Virgin, and saints,
ensconced in gilding and jewelled mosaics, gleam
through a mystic twilight.   Sculptures are forbidden by the Greek Church, but the command
against graven images is not supposed to extend
to flat surfaces or bas-reliefs.   The choir is raised
a few feet above the nave, and separated from it
by a balustrade of exquisite marbles.   The gold
Ikonostas, or screen, shuts off the " holy of ho-

lies" by two massive silver doors ; in it are eight colossal pillars, six of malachite and two of lapis lazuli—not solid, however, but laid on iron, as no such solid blocks exist in these materials. Between these pillars in the gilded screen are inserted mosaic pictures of saints. Many other beautiful pictures adorn the walls, all by Russian artists, and one exquisitely fine mosaic, representing a head of the Saviour, is studded with diamonds, the largest of which cost seven thousand pounds sterling. In fact, every available point is filled with mosaics or paintings—around the domes, the brackets for candles, as well as the walls.

In connection with them I will relate an anecdote hitherto unknown. A celebrated artist, president of one of the highest art-academies in Italy, was engaged to paint six pictures that now ornament the vault of one of the cupolas. One of the subjects selected was the Annunciation, and was enlivened by the presence of a host of little angels who floated in the upper air in the innocence of their conventional nudity. When the synod of priests visited the artist's studio to inspect the finished work, they admired everything except the undress of the infants, which they declared inadmissible. The artist protested, but in vain : the angels must conform to the regulations of religious art or be excommunicated. Accordingly, on the next visit of the synod they appeared in full celestial millinery, with broad blue ribbons and shreds of vapory costume. The work was pronounced satisfactory ; the pictures were hung under the supervision of the artist, but before he left the church they had lost their worldly tissues and circulated again unencumbered around their invisible trapeze. He had painted their draperies in *gouache*, but, to carry out his own just ideas, he washed them off before elevating the pictures to the vaulted dome ; and the then distant critics were never the wiser !

This superb church may well be considered the supreme effort of modern architecture ; unlike all other great cathedrals, which were the crystallization of centuries, it was the work of only forty years, under command of the Emperor Nicholas, who did more than all his predecessors to beautify his capital. In order to secure the safety of the foundation, forests of piles were driven into the marshy ground on which it stands, followed by great blocks of granite : and yet it gradually sinks.

Through the kindness of the lady whose acquaintance we made on the *Constantin*, we obtained privileged places within the choir, one Sunday morning, during an important ceremonial. The superb *tenue* of the priests, the marvellous singing and the devoutness of the worshippers, made a profound impression on us all ; but I may better attempt to describe a similar and more elaborate service in the Kazan cathedral, where also our friend conducted us.   This edifice, also supported on piles, is built in imitation of St. Peter's at Rome, with exterior colonnades like embracing arms.   The interior is sumptuous, though less so than St. Isaac's, and the rich surfaces are broken by flag-draped monuments and the keys of many fortresses hanging on the walls.   Among the tombs is that of General Kutusof, erected on the spot where he knelt in prayer before setting out to meet Napoleon in 1812.

The service that we attended there was conducted by the metropolitan bishop, one of the triad of bishops in the empire.   Long before the hour, the vast interior was filled with a standing or kneeling crowd—for no seats are permitted in Russian churches, except by special favor at some unobtrusive point ; nor is the use of fans allowed. Preceded by Miss M., we took our places in the choir, and chairs were provided for us only a few feet from the doors of the Ikonostas ; thus we

had a full view of the entire scene. Each person
on entering brought a taper and slowly approached a shrine ; then he knelt, bowed his head
to the marble pavement, and crossed himself repeatedly ; he lighted his candle, and set it up in
one of the large silver stands provided for that
purpose. Again kneeling, he touched his head to
the pavement and retired with face towards the
altar, continuing his prostrations and crosses during the entire service. There are no inquisitive
gazings around, and no beggars pausing in their
prayers to ask alms ; but a fixed earnestness that
evidently proceeds from deep religious feeling.
Meanwhile the choristers, in white surplices with
light-blue collars and cuffs, took their places on
each side of the Ikonostas : on this occasion the
choirs of two cathedrals were engaged. Instrumental music is forbidden in the Greek Church,
but the old hymns are most wonderful ; many of
them were brought long ago from Rome, but are

now forgotten there. Through the open doors of
the Ikonostas we saw the altar blazing with light ;
the priests, archimandrites, and deacons, twenty-
four in all, in dazzling vestments of cloth of gold
reaching to the feet, with chains and suspended
crosses, far more graceful than those of Catholic
priests, and more beautiful in quality. The dignity of the wearers is enhanced by their long,
flowing, ringleted hair, parted in the middle of the
forehead ; and with their patriarchal beards and
refined Eastern features they might serve as models for prophets and apostles. The Titianesque
reddish-gold hair of some of them accorded well
with the vestments. Some of the robes were decorated with jewels, especially the silver robe of the
bishop, who also wore a high-crowned jewelled
cap with a gold cross above it. He was a little
old man, feeble with the weight of eighty-two
years, and required assistants on either side when
he advanced to the edge of the dais and returned

many times to the altar, while he read aloud,
prayed, knelt. and crossed himself, and again with
a lighted symbolic candle in either hand blessed
the kneeling people.

The solos of the Litany were intoned by a dea-
con whose *basso profundo* of incredible power
resounded like the notes of a great organ to the
remotest end and all through the domes of the
vast building. These voices are peculiar to Russia; they are sought for through distant provinces,
and receive large remuneration. A very earnest
and frequent refrain is "*Gospodimi pomilui*"
("Lord, have mercy on us"), in which choristers
join, and prolong the last syllable like the sigh of
an Æolian harp. The most solemn moment of all
was when the priests, archimandrites, and deacons
all retired within the sanctuary, the portals silently
closed, and the people knelt during the transub-
stantiation; then the doors were thrown open,
and the whole hierarchy, in their superb vestments,

"gold in sunlight against gold in shadow," walked
forth to the chanting and singing of the most
perfect church-music I have ever heard; deep as
thunder, yet most harmonious in tone, the bass
rose and poised on waves of grand *crescendo*,
around which floated and fell the soft silvery ca-
dence of the sopranos and intermediate parts.

It is to the honor of the Greek Church that it
has never been intolerant of other creeds, and al-
lows public worship in every form. It has been
said that "Toleration" Street would be an appro-
priate title for the Nevski Prospekt from the number of churches of various persuasions it contains.

### PALACES AND MUSEUMS.

One of the most pleasant things to do in St.
Petersburg is to visit the palace of Tsarskoé-Selo,
a stately pleasure-dome decreed by Catherine the
Great. We went by rail fifteen miles out to a
village adjoining the park, where we obtained tick-

ets of admission, and thence a carriage conveyed us
through the extensive grounds to the palace. The
façade is elaborately adorned with statues, carvings, and vases, which, with the pedestals and capitals of the columns, were originally covered with
gold. In the course of a few years the rigors of
winter made serious havoc with this decoration,
and Murray says that the persons who repaired
it offered the Empress fifty thousand pounds
sterling for the fragments of gold-leaf, to which
she disdainfully replied, "*Je ne suis pas dans
l'usage de vendre mes vieilles hardes.*" There are
no traces of this lavish ornamentation left except
on the cupolas of the chapel, the interior of which
is painted in bright blue and gold, displeasing to
the eye. But the ingenuity of even that reckless
age was taxed to the utmost in the long succession of salons, all arranged as if for an immediate
court pageant. Gold (not gilded) ceilings, silk-
hung walls, floors of costliest inlaid woods in

graceful designs—one of polished ebony inlaid with figures of mother-of-pearl, and walls incrusted with lapis lazuli : a Chinese room of choicest Celestial furniture : a banqueting-room with a dado nine feet high covered with plates of gold ; the walls of the chamber of Catherine the Great laid in fine porcelain tiles, and supported by pilasters of blue glass, with priceless rock-crystal chandeliers, articles of *vertu*, tables and *tazzas* of malachite and lapis lazuli, so profuse as to defy memory and re-cital. There are two ball-rooms, in each of which is a collection of the rarest porcelain vases placed in circular tiers which extend from floor to ceiling; the letter E. for *Ekaterina*, inscribed on each vase.

The gem of all is the Amber Room. Its lofty walls are entirely covered with that exquisite material in architectural designs ; some of them represent the arms of Catherine united with those of Frederick the Great, by whom the amber was presented ; amber groups of figures rest upon an amber ground. Shreds of amber in beads and pipes convey no idea of the soft gleams of mellow light in this poetic room, which but for the realism of some of the designs would seem to have been stolen from a supernatural realm. It was the most unique object we saw in Russia. Even the chairs were of amber, with seats of pale-yellow brocade ; and a set of amber chessmen stood on an amber field.

We were interested in the full-length portraits of the Romanoffs, all indicative of their characteristics. The portraits of Alexander I. and Alexander II. are particularly pleasing ; their commanding figures and fine faces express the best qualities of the dynasty, without its faults. The artist who depicted the sensuous beauty of the intellectual, arrogant, unscrupulous Catherine II., who was not a Romanoff, took good care to put her evil traits in the background.

The splendor of the state apartments finds

antithesis in the small, almost monastic rooms of that excellent monarch Alexander I., which are sacredly preserved precisely as he left them for a tour to his southern provinces, where death put an end to his beneficent reign. In one corner is a camp bedstead, on a table a few modest toilet appurtenances, a hand-mirror in a green morocco frame, brushes and comb of the simplest sort, an ordinary pocket-handkerchief, a worn and faded uniform. Very unostentatious also are the living-rooms in a small palace built for him in his youth, but occasionally occupied by the present imperial family. The high and mighty personages whose frequent fate it is

"to be perked up in a glistening grief
And wear a golden sorrow"

are often pleased to relax their pose and become simple ladies and gentlemen.

In this palace there is little furniture or decora-

tion of intrinsic value, and even trifles that would
be banished from ordinary drawing-rooms as insignificant. But there are children's toys, photographs, and portraits—not for show, but for family
love; and in a large hall is a high inclined plane
of polished wood for the children to play at "to-
bogganing" within doors. The Emperor's writ-
ing-table was like that of a man of business. In
glass cases around one of the rooms are models
of cavalry regiments, beautifully executed for the
Emperor Nicholas, and many paintings of military
manœuvres.

A fusillade of rain prevented us from any extended walk or drive through the stately pleas-
aunce in summer green, where are several charming caprices, such as a Chinese village, a Dutch
cow-house, artificial ruins, a fountain after Greuze's
picture of "La Cruche cassée," and many others.

The Arsenal of Tsarskoé-Selo is a superb collection of armor and antique standards amassed

by many sovereigns ; prominent among them are two dazzling saddles, every part of which, together with the bridles, are covered with brilliants.

Thence we drove to the village of Pavolsk, where there is another palace, and all sorts of picturesque adjuncts which approaching twilight prevented us from seeing.

We dined at a fashionable restaurant there, to the music of an excellent orchestra. We were anxious to hear the National Hymn on its native heath, but never had an opportunity, because it is played only on special occasions and involves the ceremony of the whole audience standing through the performance. One of the dishes at our dinner was a good cabbage-soup, called *stchi*, served with sour cream ; another was *rastigàe*, patties of the isinglass and flesh of sturgeon ; also a very delicate "sweet,"—something between jelly and ice.

Whence the far-famed Hermitage derives its

name one fails to perceive on the face of it, for
it is neither remote nor secluded ; as well might
the Louvre be called a monastic cell. But the
versatile Catherine built the original as a retreat
from state cares in the society of literati and artists, and the modern edifice, finished forty years
ago, preserves the inappropriate name.

No museum in Europe is so beautiful or so
costly. A very gorgeous lackey received our cards
at the entrance, and two others, equally bedizened,
stood at the foot of the stately flight of marble
steps. Sixteen red-granite monoliths and ten
giants of gray granite support the vestibule, and
numerous statues of artists fill niches in the
walls. At the head of the three flights which
compose the stairway are two magnificent candelabra stands of violet jasper from Siberia. The
decorations of galleries and corridors only faintly
indicate the wealth of the empire in marbles, malachite, lapis lazuli, crystals, precious stones, and

gold. The pictures in the gallery are set off by crimson-silk hangings on the walls; the floors, of polished wood-mosaic, are uniform in color, without lights and shades, and therefore not intrusive on the paintings. Rich crimson - silk - covered chairs and sofas offer rest, and vases and *tazzas* of jasper and onyx stand upon tables of pink porphyry and malachite. There are fifteen hundred pictures, beautifully arranged and well lighted. The Spanish collection seemed to me the best out of Spain; but while rich in specimens of Murillo, it fails to rival the Madrid gallery in Velasquez portraits. There are several Raphaels, Titians, and Tintorettos, but not the masterpieces of those painters, and on the whole the Italian school does not compare with that in Florence. The French pictures are numerous and beautiful, but the Flemish and Dutch collection is the finest of all.

However, my opinion, rapidly formed, is offered as that of an amateur, not a critic; for weeks of

study would be required to know thoroughly
these treasures, to which all the most celebrated
painters in Europe have contributed. The room
of Russian pictures is very interesting, because
national in design, and novel in subject; the artists receive much encouragement from the government, and when they indicate talent are sent
off with pensions to study in Paris and Rome. It
was unfortunate for us that several private galleries were closed for the summer, especially in
Moscow, and we thus missed seeing some of the
most celebrated Russian creations.

The numismatic collection, which is extremely
rich and valuable, contains rare coins from Greece
and from all the ancient provinces of Russia,
many of them earlier than the period of dies, being
merely bits of metal chopped from the mass.
About one thousand English specimens of the
reigns of Canute and Ethelred were excavated in
Russia, and doubtless served, as did the large

numbers found in Scandinavia, for commerce in furs.

There is a long series of rooms filled with gems, mosaics, precious manuscripts, engraved stones, and cameos, and a curious collection excavated at Kertch in the Crimea, which was a point of Greek civilization 500 B.C.   Here are crowns, weapons, and ornaments of gold which had been untouched more than two thousand years ; a priestess of Ceres, who was buried with all her ornaments and four horses, the trappings of which remain ; innumerable bracelets, necklaces, brooches, etc., enriched with enamel, filigree, and precious stones, and finer than all modern work-manship ; gold stirrups and bits ; exquisite ob-jects in colored glass, an art which the Venetians learned from Greece at a later period ; a beautiful head-ornament of ears of wheat ; and silver *re-poussé* vases and drinking-cups, unrivalled in the world.   In truth this collection of classic jewelry is far more rich and varied than that of the Vatican or the British Museum. Amid all this paraphernalia of beauty and of vanity is a small wooden comb inscribed, " A present from Sister" ! There is also an electrum vase with *repoussé* figures of Scythians mending their weapons, one having a tooth extracted, a third his wounds dressed, and all costumed like the Russian peasantry of to-day—the shirt outside the trousers, and the trousers inside the boots ! Hard study for many weeks would scarcely serve to familiarize one with the treasures of the Hermitage ; but, alas ! our

> " bird of Time had but a little way to flutter,
> And the Bird was on the wing" !

We turned into the gallery of Peter the Great, and encountered an effigy of the Iron Tsar, startlingly realistic and very like his numerous portraits, with pronounced Muscovite features, coal-black

hair and mustache, and wide-open eyes gazing at
the relics of his mundane existence.   He is seated
in a chair, dressed in a faded and worn blue-silk
doublet and hose embroidered by the peasant-wife
whom he loved so well,—"my heart's friend," as
he called her,—who retained her influence by not
changing her native simplicity or putting on airs
after she became Tsarina.   Peter's massive canes
stand near him, and he looks as if he were quite
ready to seize one of them according to his wont
and lay it across the shoulders of servant or officer
who might offend him.   A heavy iron one among
the number might well leave a lasting souvenir
of the irascible owner.   There are more credita-
ble tokens of his personality in telescopes, mathe-
matical instruments, turning-lathes, and implements for wood-carving ; also a wax cast of his
face, taken while he lived.

In the small palace which he had built for himself, the first house on the marshes of the Neva,

the furniture is principally the work of his hands—
wardrobes, tables, arm-chairs, and a clock, carved
with taste and skill. A wax model in a glass case
in this gallery of the Hermitage represents an
exceedingly quaint little body who was his house-
keeper in Holland; and a pole seven feet high
shows his own stature. Here also are scores of
other cases filled with every conceivable device for
the display of diamonds, rubies, emeralds, and
sapphires; snuff-boxes, jewel-coffers, rings, necklaces, watches, gold goblets, in endless variety; imperial crowns; Potemkin's glittering plume, presented by the Sultan; Suvaroff's, given by the
Shah; two watches in the shape of ducks, one in
the form of an egg; a small parrot carved from an
emerald; bouquets of flowers made entirely of
precious stones; several jewelled walking-sticks
that belonged to Catherine; and a mechanical
clock, also her property, but now out of order,
which represents a gilded peacock of life-size,

whose tail when expanded was studded with sapphires, emeralds, and diamonds ; a cock that with
blazing crest flapped his wings, an owl that rolled
his onyx eyes, and a brilliant grasshopper devour-
ing an agate mushroom ; fine ivory carvings ;
pocket-books of tortoise-shell studded with sapphires and rubies ; and countless other costly combinations of jewels, which are not merely marvels
of workmanship but are associated with all the
illustrious names of the last two centuries.

There is a little cottage of two rooms on the
Neva which Peter occupied before the erection of
the house alluded to above. The small room
where he ate and slept is now a chapel, completely
lined with pictures of saints in gilded shrines, the
most important one being a repulsive image of
the Saviour, which accompanied Peter wherever he
went. It is believed to have wrought many mira-
cles, and to be potent against all ills of humanity.
The day we were there we noticed a young

moujik kneeling opposite this image ; with incessant crossings he prostrated himself on the marble
floor, which was swept by his long dark hair ; but
his trembling lips and streaming eyes betrayed
some stronger emotion than that of ordinary
prayer : his gaze was riveted on the unresponsive
picture with a pleading agony that meant life or
death. We walked slowly around the chapel, and
then went out to see the boat which Peter himself
created ; we lingered in the porch and watched the
devotees who thronged to the shrine : and still he
knelt and wept and kissed the sacred stones, as if
his utter abandonment of woe *must* wrest from the
symbol or from its antitype a promise or a conso-
lation. What cruel reality pressed upon him we
could not know ; was it the menaced life of one
he loved, or was it—Siberia ? We could not in-
trude upon him, nor could we command his language ; but we shall never forget that abject peasant on the banks of the Neva.

Very near this point stand the high battle-mented walls of the fortress of St. Peter and St. Paul, which is also a prison, and contains the mint, and a cathedral whose pyramidal spire, covered with gold and surmounted, as usual, by an angel and a cross, is the highest in Russia and towers conspicuously above the city. All the Tsars since the time of Peter are buried here, as before they were buried in Moscow. The walls are covered with military trophies, flags, keys of fortresses, etc., the tokens of various foreign conquests.

The emperors' tombs are of white marble without effigies. Above each is a sacred image set with diamonds. The one above Peter the Great represents his stature and breadth at his birth, $5\frac{1}{4}$ inches by $19\frac{1}{4}$; the image of St. Paul above the Emperor Paul serving a like purpose. Commemorative wreaths and flowers lay upon the tomb of Alexander II., whose assassination still pervades

the capital with a tremor of pain and foreboding.
In the museum of imperial carriages, which we
visited the same day, there was nothing so impressive as the one he occupied when the fatal shot
was fired. It is a closed carriage of the ordinary
style, lined with dark-blue silk. The first bullet
tore open half the back and killed the footman ;
as every one remembers, the emperor was shot
after he stepped out of the vehicle to support his
valued servant. A commemorative chapel is now
in process of erection on the spot.

This museum is one of the essential sights of
St. Petersburg. The lower floor is occupied by
the ordinary travelling and town equipages of the
court, which of course are as handsome and luxurious as modern art can make them. A flight of
stairs lined with beautiful Gobelin tapestries leads
to the second story, where forty or fifty immense
vehicles create a perfect blaze of splendor. They
are all completely covered with gold, even to the

spokes of the wheels, which revolve around axles dazzling with Siberian jewels. They are all lined with red-silk velvet; the panels of several are beautifully painted by French artists, and those belonging to the empresses bear the arms of Russia incrusted with diamonds. The coachman who had the honor of conveying Catherine the Great sat on a box upheld by carved and gilded eagles ; the back of the vehicle is guarded by St. George and the Dragon, and above the roof blazes a jewelled crown. Another, made for the same empress, is painted on gold ground with allegorical designs,—Venus leaving her bath ; Catherine as a deity from Olympus, bringing Peace and Plenty, etc.,—and the velvet interior is decorated with rich Spanish point-lace. Another contained a small stove and a card-table ; and some of them would hold ten or twelve occupants. They require at least eight horses, and the Russians frequently drive four or five abreast. The harnesses and saddles exhibit the same lavishness of gold and color, with most elaborate finish and inter-mixture of jewels. Coachmen and footmen are nearly covered with gold lace on their green, blue, or red velvet attire at the coronation of an emperor, when all these emblazoned carriages and trappings are sent off to Moscow, to figure in the pageant. The oldest of them are without springs, are hung very high, and are attached by straps to poles twenty feet long and of great thickness.

Again our favorite Tsar, Peter, presents himself through the sledge made by his ingenious hands. It is merely a square box painted some dark color, with mica windows and one hard, uncom-fortable seat; a small wooden trunk behind held his clothes and provisions for the journey to Arch-angel. No Sybarite was the iron-willed Tsar.

The long twilights of July afforded us charming drives in the extensive public parks on the islands in the river, where we found many sylvan nooks and picturesque bridges over streams studded with fanciful chalets, each with its own pretty garden. The trees are generally firs and birch, smaller than those in Norway ; but there are also fine oaks.

---

I have outlined with rapid pen only a few of the salient features of this fascinating capital ; but my modest pages approach their limit, and I must yet present a brief kaleidoscopic view of the ancient and beloved city of the Tsars—" Holy Moscow."

THE KREMLIN—MOSCOW.

# CHAPTER II.

WHEN the Emperor Nicholas decreed a railway between St. Petersburg and Moscow
for military convenience, and with pen in hand
drew a straight line, which left out all villages
and towns *en route*, he builded better than he
knew, or cared, for the benefit of future tourists.
A more flat and desolate intervening country
would be difficult to find anywhere; even more
dreary is it than the desert plateau between Bur-
gos and Madrid. Therefore one loses nothing by
taking the night-train to Moscow, which starts
about eight o'clock.

We had secured a private compartment the previous day by a few rubles supplementary to the

salary of some prominent official, who greeted us with the high consideration always awarded to such disinterested action. Our small *salon,* furnished with two tables, was convertible into a comfortable bedroom.

The road, which was constructed by an American engineer, is remarkably smooth, and the carriages are luxurious. The stations, standing in oases of trees and gardens, are built of red brick and white stone, and are the most spacious and handsome I have ever seen. In each one is a gay little shop for the sale of national trifles, sculptured wooden crosses, morocco slippers embroidered in silver and gold, Circassian belts, knives in *niello* work, etc. Waiters in full dress serve excellent refreshments, and the buffets offer fair wines, beer, *kvas,* a sort of fruit-syrup, *lestofka,* a spirit flavored with black-currant leaves, *vodka,* which is not a fiery liquid—in small quantities—and more pleasant than brandy, besides all the curious "appetizers," called *zakuska.* Half an hour or more is allowed at the principal stopping-places, and there are frequent pauses of ten minutes, which give opportunity to scan the coming and going pilgrims as they frequented the stations. As we approached Moscow we noticed officers in dashing uniforms; long-bearded merchants; Tartars or Armenians; Russian peasants in long caftans and long hair; women with bright-colored handkerchiefs tied at the back of their heads; a little better class sparkling with chains, bracelets, and all sorts of showy jewelry. No one hastens, for there are three warning bells, and no confusion prevails.

The distance to Moscow is about fourteen hours, and in the luminous summer night we had ample opportunity to study the monotonous and dreary landscape. Hour after hour the scene repeats itself: now and then appears a cluster of miserable wooden cabins, with a few vegetables struggling

out of the earth; no farms, no paths, no inclos-
ures; sometimes a small white church with green

RUSSIAN COSTUME.

cupola indicates that souls as well as bodies inhabit those pitiful abodes. It is said, however,

that the peasants are a contented, good-humored race and may be very merry on occasion, especially when in the winter snows, well wrapped in sheep-skins, they disport like polar bears. But the intolerable cold and darkness of six months of the year and the prostrating heat of three months more must dishearten, and the consequence is a continuous flow of population into the cities, where employment of some sort is readily obtained, not only to support life, but also to pay the tax to the *commune,* which since the emancipation of the serfs takes the place of that formerly given to the nobles or the State.

By the terms of the emancipation law the serfs were divided into *communes,* which possess the land in common, under a local government ; but any member of the *commune* may readily obtain from it permission to seek employment in one of the cities, and to pay his tribute in money instead of in labor on the land. We heard from several sources that the servants are incorrigible pilferers (except the Tartars, who are perfectly honest) ; but

RUSSIAN PEASANT.

as an offset they are good-humored, respectful, and obedient. There was a story told many years ago of a soldier on guard in the Winter Palace when it took fire and the whole interior was consumed. A priest who was hurrying from the chapel with some of its sacred vessels warned him to quit his post. "I wait orders," said the man. The priest hurriedly absolved him, and he stood sturdily at his post and was burned to death.

The monotony of the road to Moscow is broken twice by long bridges over streams which wander away through endless plains and between dismal forests, howling in winter with wolves and bears, till they unite with the Volga and are finally lost in the Caspian Sea. About ten o'clock in the morning we passed several rather pretty villages, masses of dark trees, and finally, through the veil of thin, quivering haze, we caught sight of the burnished domes, the pinnacles, crosses, and polychromatic colors of the ancient city of the Tsars. How gay was our excitement! how hypocritical our assumed composure! *Moscow :* so far from home it sounded! so like a bit from the Arabian Nights it looked!

The conventionalities of the railway station and the appearance of a hybrid Russo-English *valet de place* from the hotel dispelled the illusion, and we were soon whirling through the labyrinthine streets, which in their confusion of geometry and mad festivity of color resembled a kaleidoscope out of order, until we arrived at the Slavianski Bazaar. This edifice is not a place of merchandise, but a comfortable hotel, whose appointments, though composite of Russian and German, adapt themselves to all seasonable requirements. There are no *tables d'hôte* in Russia, but for a party of travellers dinner *à la carte* is always more agreeable. There is an English manager, who attends very civilly to his guests. Two porters stand like caryatides at the entrance-door when not engaged in opening and shutting carriages; their dress is like that of the guards on

the railway—white gloves, full plaited dark woollen caftans belted around the waist and reaching
to the knees, where they meet the loose high
boots universal in the lower classes ; but unlike
the guards they wear high *evasés*, cloth caps with
the æsthetic appendage of peacock-feathers all
around the front.

Our suite of rooms had a balcony which over-
looked a square thoroughly Oriental, save for the
lack of turbans and burnouses.

This part of Moscow is the *Kitai Gorod*, or
Chinese City, so called because within its walls
merchants formerly sought shelter for the treasures they brought from China and other foreign
sources.   The Slavianski Bazaar was probably
a prominent point of traffic.   On one side of the
square were several churches ; one with clusters of
pale-green cupolas surmounted by Greek crosses,
and bell-towers shaped like bulbs ; another, more
distant, gleaming in various colors of red, blue,

green, and silver, like the scales of the fabled dragon; in front, the turrets and buttresses of the

WINE SELLER—MOSCOW MARKET.

wall of the *Kitai Gorod;* and between these a market-place crowded with men in blue shirts,

red shirts, and patriarchal beards ; a few women
in motley wear ; vendors of fish, vegetables, and
wine, with baskets on their heads ; rude, unpainted
carts, and shaggy, long-haired horses slightly har-
nessed with ropes, and a murmur in the air of
strange, soft syllables.

The Russian language is very pleasant to the ear
and pictorial to the eye ; but its grammar, which
has no article, bristles with declinations, inflections,
and inversions which no foreigner but Mezzofanti
could conquer and only Mark Twain could justly
describe.     Breakfast was served in our sitting-
room—*tchai slamonum* and strawberries, of course ;
and our brief vocabulary, here as everywhere,
proved an essential acquisition, for the servants,
with one exception, spoke nothing but Russ ;
our chambermaid also was a native and knew
only four French words, but made up the deficit
with smiles.

### THE STREETS.

We soon started for a drive, under the leadership of Evanson, the *valet de place,* who was henceforth our constant attendant. It is best to engage a carriage by the week ; for although the pavements are as bad as they well can be, and there is little pleasure in the movement, yet the distances are too great for ladies to walk, and at all events they should never walk unattended.

There is as great a contrast between the two capitals of Russia as between its two zones of climate and cultivation. St. Petersburg rises from a flat and marshy delta apparently more water than land ; broad rivers and a sea menace its existence ; its wide, right-angled streets, modern palaces, and general pomp of classic imitation are not in harmony with gilded spires and domes of Muscovite antiquity. Moscow, which is about twenty-five miles in circumference, rises on gently-undulating hills around which glides a small sinuous river; the irregular streets are built in two concentric zones, the interior of which is the older and more picturesque one. In the centre, on a yet more elevated hill, stands the Kremlin, visible from every point within the horizon, and on all sides the sky-line is pierced by sparkling domes, cupolas, spires, and pinnacles, with an effect like aërial *chevaux de frise* of gold and silver. After the great conflagration in 1812 the city was re-built on the same tortuous lines, with little change of general aspect except that more gardens were introduced and the houses were more decorated. The Kremlin was much less injured than the city at large, and thus the venerable city retains, except in its modern outstretching boulevards, its ancient prestige. It is the revered Mecca of the Russian peasant, who as soon as he catches sight from afar of the golden cross on the Ivan tower falls on his knees with patriotic devotion.

GAME VENDOR—MOSCOW MARKET.

It is less than two hundred years since the influence of Western Europe was first known in Russia, and thus far the traditions and customs of the East are not effaced. Long centuries of Byzantine civilization, which even under Tartar rule was preserved in the convent fortresses, have impressed upon the people great faith in their religion, fidelity to the Tsars, and love for the fatherland. All these elements of stability promise well for the future greatness of the empire ; and to these may be added the material dependence of each portion upon the others. The grain-lands of the South, the forests of the North, the sea-coasts of both for the industrial interior, form a mutual and permanent bond of necessity.

Only after many days does the eye accustom itself to the bizarre and marvellous variety of form and color in Moscow. Here stands a palace with imposing iron portals painted in red and gold ; there, a white church with a constellation of stars

on the blue ground of its dome; next, a cluster
of yellow wooden tenements, then a family mansion with profuse pillars ; again, we pass an open
court or garden entered through a wrought-iron
trellised gateway that stands between green and
white columns, and within we see a convent, or a
church, or a private dwelling, with splashes of red
roof, blue roof, green roof, or gilded cupolas :—
as if a mad painter had shaken a gigantic palette
full of color over the entire city. Add to this the
ornate signs above the shops and the same gay
simulacra as at St. Petersburg of fruits, vegetables,
wines, etc. The shrines for holy images with
perpetual lamps before them are more profuse,
and the genuflections and signs of the cross more
noticeable, perhaps because the streets are not so
wide and the crowd is larger.

There are fewer foreigners in Moscow, and odd
costumes are frequent. Now and then a Persian
or an Armenian in embroidered fez and jacket

and creamy silk vest strides with slippered feet along the pavement, or a turbaned Circassian, girt with silver belt from which hangs a scimitar and a yataghan. White-bearded old peasants from the country with serious blue eyes would pose as Abrahams to the delight of an artist, and the hand-worked dresses of the girls with lavish strings of colored beads are extremely tasteful.

We took a drive one Sunday afternoon to the Petrovski Park, and came upon the Sax Garden, where there was a fine band and restaurant, and a crowd of pleasure-seekers as gay as parrots and peacocks. One costume was a high, gold-embroidered cap, and a black silk dress with scarlet sleeves, to which were added gold chains, brooches, and necklaces enough to fit out a jeweller's window. But such attire is exceptional; the usual dress is cosmopolitan, with national variations. Our *valet de place*, who perhaps had his own interest in the matter, conducted us one day to a

small shop of purely Caucasian silks and ornaments, the master of which was a Persian, and
in his becoming native costume a superb specimen of Oriental manly beauty, with tragic face
and reverent courtesy of manner. His creamy
silk shawls were as fascinating as himself, and we
made several purchases at prices lower than he
asked, though not without a feeling that it was
almost an insult to his Grandeur to ask a reduc-
tion on the wares he condescended to hand over
to our Commonplaces. After this, one of my
party, whose blue eyes see all in the world that
is beautiful and good and nothing that is ugly
or evil, vanished every day for half an hour, under
the protection of Evanson, ostensibly to buy a
Bagdad shawl or some bit of Eastern trumpery,
but actually, I believe, for the sake of seeing this
Persian Magnificence lay his hand on his heart and
say in soft syllables, with a voice as deep-toned and
sonorous as a Moscow bell, "To *you*, my lady,

I *would* give it for ten rubles ; but, alas ! I *cannot* for less than fifteen ! Nevertheless, accept it for twelve !"

The bells of Moscow ! There may exist such musical intonations elsewhere, but I have never heard them. Every morning at an early hour the bells in the churches near the Slavianski Bazaar lifted their grand voices, not suddenly, in stunning avalanche of sound, but in single successive notes in the same diapason, which filled the air with harmonious pulsations, deep and thrilling as those of a mighty organ. All other bells, even festive bells in other lands, are a jangle and a wrangle forever hereafter,—excepting " Big Ben " of Westminster and St. Mark's in Venice, which in their melodious resonance are akin to those of Moscow. The great bell of the Ivan tower is unequalled in size as well as in *timbre ;* it was brought from Novgorod the Great, where it once called the population to arms when the Muscovite

IVAN TOWER, KREMLIN—MOSCOW.

Grand Dukes threatened their freedom.   There are thirty-two more bells in the Ivan tower, two of them made of silver, and the oldest one bears the date of 1550.   There are 345 churches in Moscow, and as doubtless they all have bells, the flood of melodious sound on Christmas and Easter morning may be imagined.

At the foot of the Ivan tower stands on a low granite pedestal the colossal Tsar Kolokol, or King of Bells, which weighs about five hundred and fifty thousand pounds.   Its date is unknown, for it fell and was recast several times, and each time gained essentially in weight.   In 1733 it was last recast, and the ladies of Moscow commemorated the occasion by throwing into the liquid metal many jewels and gold and silver ornaments, which probably weakened its strength, for it fell again five years later, and remained half-buried for a century.   This tower of brass with walls two feet thick, capable of holding twenty-five or thirty men, will probably never again fulfil its mission as a bell, but now poses as a monument and a failure.

The clustered bells that ring successive notes in the same diapason remind me of an anecdote of a certain princess who was accustomed to entertain her guests by the instrumental performance of a number of her serfs, who were trained, according to a prevailing custom, to sound each his single note in the proper place in the harmony. One evening the musicians were not forthcoming as usual, and on the princess being asked the reason, she replied, "I am sorry that you can have no music to-night, but my C sharp has received forty lashes of the knout to-day, and is therefore unable to sound his note."

### THE KREMLIN.

The Kremlin, or ancient citadel, dating back of the XV. century, was repeatedly destroyed by fire in its earlier days, and has existed in its present form only one hundred and fifty years. Its crenelated walls, pierced by five great archways of entrance, embrace a triangular space of two square miles, and are flanked by enormous towers of every conceivable shape and size, round and square, light and graceful as minarets, or solid as bastions, surmounted by steep scaly roofs, brilliant as the hues of a tropical serpent. Below the ramparts lie verdant terraces, around the foot of which winds the lovely Moskva River. Formerly, watchmen on these battlements were constantly on the look-out, and when they saw clouds of dust sweeping over the flat plains of the south they knew that the Tartar hordes of the Crimea were at hand with devastating purpose. Then the great bell of the Ivan tower sounded the call of warning, and every one fled for safety to the fortified monasteries or the palace, at whose gates the wild horsemen battered in vain. The Kremlin, which is the arsenal of the army, the centre of the most sacred churches and of the royal palaces, is the Acropolis of Russia, and has been compared to the Alhambra. But the Alhambra has no such opulence of clustered domes and pinnacles, no such lavishment of golden reflections; the shadows of a gifted and injured people rest upon its massive bastions ; the last sigh of Boabdil lingers in the Hall of Lions, and modern restorations of its delicate polychromatic tracery cannot chase the phantoms of sad sultanas, whose lutes once vibrated to laughter and the silvery fall of fountains. The Kremlin has no similar pathos in its history. The race that created it is the race of to-day, in full progress of development, and its reverence for the past combines with the love and hope of the present. I believe that one reason why our tour through Norway and Russia was so full of enjoyment was because we were not called upon to sigh over mouldering palaces and be-poetized ruins.

SPASSKI (REDEEMER) GATE—KREMLIN.

The most grandiose gate leading into the Kremlin is the Spasski (Redeemer) Gate, so called because above the arch of entrance on the inner side is a sacred picture of the Saviour, which is one of the most revered in the city. No one, from Tsar to peasant, ever goes by without saluting it, and strangers are warned to follow that example—not only to uncover the head, but to leave it uncovered until they have passed through the deep archway : a requisition which, when the thermometer is ten or fifteen degrees below zero, must be rather conducive to sudden influenza. There is a legend that once when the Tartars attacked the Kremlin, such a mist came suddenly from the picture that they were unable to find the entrance. Criminals formerly executed in the large square outside always offered it their last prayers.

There is another gate called the Nicholas, over which is suspended a miraculous image of St. Nicholas. Napoleon ordered the destruction of this tower, but it escaped with only a cleft that extended to the frame of the picture, and not even the glass before it, or the hanging-lamp, was injured.　After passing through the Spasski Gate we are on the elevated esplanade that overlooks the city, and surrounded by palaces, monasteries, and churches from which rise fantasic minarets and arrowy stems supporting crown-like golden domes, and clusters of larger domes which from certain angles reflect on their burnished surfaces clouds above and trees below.　Beyond spreads the broad panorama.

From the summit of the Ivan tower, which we ascended, there is a view as dazzling as a scene of enchantment.　The eye sweeps over gardens, buildings with gay-colored roofs, and the thousand domes and countless Greek crosses which group in dark rich masses or spring in airy brightness under the play of sunshine and shadow.

## THE KREMLIN—PALACES.

We went every day to the Kremlin, and the days were all too few. We had only ten ; but they began early and ended late, and fortunately the usual warmth of summer was tempered by a daily shower. We awoke early each morning to the sound of those glorious bells, and we always sprang to the balcony to assure ourselves that the *mise-en-scène* had not vanished in the night.

We passed two long mornings at the Imperial Palace and the adjoining one of the ancient Tsars. Their details are fixed on my memory, but I hesitate to attempt description. The New Palace built by Nicholas presents externally a mixture of architecture quite incongruous with the Byzantine edifices around it, but the interior has all the ostentation of space resplendent with gold and color that delights the Russian eye. The vestibule is supported by the usual monoliths, which here are of gray marble, and the lofty staircase is of the same material. Two superb crystal vases stand on either side at the top, and the wall is nearly covered by a vigorous painting of the victory of Dimitry of the Don over the Tartars, in 1380—a ruinous victory, as he began with four hundred thousand men and ended with forty thousand. A good monarch, say historians, was this same Dimitry, just and kindly, but the victim of Tartar invasion at last.

From this picture we pass through ante-rooms and corridors, until we reach the chastely beautiful Hall of St. George, two hundred feet long and proportionally wide and high, all in gold and white ; the floors of exquisite marquetrie, the walls inscribed with the names in gold of the members of the Order. The crystal chandeliers hold 3,200 candles ; but the next room *en suite*, the Alexander Hall, which is only half as long, is lighted by 4,500. This superb room in pink and

gold is filled with pictures relating to the life of
St. Alexander Nevsky. Then follows the Hall of
St. Andrew, vaulted like a Gothic cathedral, with
walls of pale-blue silk and gold ; and the thrones
of the emperor and empress at the end are su-
perbly carved and gilded, with jewelled crowns
and a jewelled letter A resting above the gold-embroidered crimson velvet which cushions them ;
the dais and the steps leading to it are covered
with cloth of gold.

We proceed to other state drawing-rooms and
state bedrooms adorned with brocaded walls, jasper mantelpieces, verde-antique pilasters, mirrors
in silver frames, etc., until we are sated with modern splendor, and gladly descend by an inner passage to the ancient palace of the Tsars, which is
so fantastic and bizarre that we seem to have been
led blindfold to Ispahan or Bagdad.

I cannot picture all these most curious rooms ;
but the banqueting-room where the emperor and

empress dine the day of their coronation will suffice to give an idea of the others. The ceiling is formed of gilded vaultings which meet in the centre, and are upheld by an enormous pillar around which stands in prandial pomp, on these occasions, a massive and ancient silver service. Geometric figures of frowning colors overlie the gold of the walls, and, following the lines of the arches, dark inscriptions in old Sclavonic letters bear to a stranger's eye a mysterious menace like that of the writing on Belshazzar's wall. The newly-crowned sovereigns in the pomp of their regalia sit on thrones under a canopy of cloth of gold bordered with ermine, and drink to the health of their subjects, while crowned heads only share their repast. The highest functionaries and superior clergy are seated at side tables, always facing the imperial party.

The carpet in this room is like Persian embroideries, a wonderful massing of brilliant bits

of cloth sewed into apertures cut in the ground-
work ; the colors very bright, but quite in harmony with the principles of that sort of art.

Very interesting is the *Terem,* or suite of rooms
in the upper stories set apart for the wives and
children of the Tsars, to which the ascent is by a
narrow twisted stairway with carved stone balustrade ; the rooms are small and vaulted, ceilings
and walls overlaid with ornate and elaborate
arabesques ; red predominates in one room, blue
in another, green in a third ; frescoes intermingled
present sacred subjects, and the narrow painted
windows repeat the mural colors. The light as
it came through them was dim and cloistered even
that summer day, and must have been lugubrious
indeed to the royal ladies who were once restricted
to these narrow limits. One wonders how they
passed the interminable hours : the wife of Peter
the Great in her modest home in St. Petersburg
embroidered her husband's doublet and superin-

tended his dinner. The furniture is Asiatic in fashion, very odd but unostentatious ; a cushion and rug that lie at the foot of the uncomfortable wooden arm-chair of the Tsar Michael were worked by one of his daughters, but their barbaric combinations of color would scarcely find favor in our art-schools.

There is a charming, quaint simplicity in the ancient Romanoff house outside of the Kremlin, where we felt introduced into a princely Russian household of three centuries past. It would leave much to desire in this luxurious age, in size, light, and comfort ; but as the small, low rooms are made of carved wood, dark brown with age, they contrast restfully with the opulence of decoration in other royal abodes. It has even now a look of home life ; we could almost see the sturdy Romanoff children playing with the toys and primers which are preserved in a glass case since they were laid there two hundred years ago,—such toys and primers as our babies would laugh to scorn,—and we could fancy the grandfather of our friend Peter shuffling about in the half-worn yellow-leather slippers that have survived him, and the Tsarina complacent with her extremely coarse linen chemise—embroidered all the same—now yellow with the tints of time.

## THE KREMLIN—CHURCHES.

The most characteristic church in Moscow is the Cathedral of the Assumption, in the Kremlin, where the Tsars have always been crowned. Its dark and sumptuous interior recalls the gleaming cavern of St. Mark's, but does not, like that, stretch into mystical indistinctness. Four immense square pillars supporting the central cupola are flanked by four smaller ones. On the golden ground which covers every inch of the walls, as well as of the pillars, are depicted hundreds of sombre, archaic saints, martyrs, and even the Eternal Father in guise of an old man with sweeping white hair and beard—a pantheon of nimbussed gods whose sad, fixed eyes and extended hands seem to menace rather than bless. The lofty gold wall of the Ikonostas reaches almost to the ceiling; on its façade stand five rows of saints, one above the other, their aureoles studded with diamonds, while bracelets and necklaces of rubies, sapphires, pearls, emeralds, and amethysts sparkle around their brown necks and hands. The more uncouth in mien and color these images, the more they are esteemed; those of most ancient and holy repute are nearly black, like the Madonnas of St. Luke. Their accompaniments of burning lamps, candles, jewels, and gold seem little removed from pagan idolatry; but we remember that these symbols appeal to the imagination : that flame is a token of the presence of the Holy Spirit, and lavishness of ornament bestowed represents the abnegation of the givers.

But although the first effect of these Russian churches dazzles the eye and kindles the fancy, we recur with increased admiration to the "petrified music" of Gothic architecture, the perspective of "long-drawn aisle and fretted vault," and the personality of sculptured saints and apostles.

As an example of the realistic impression of the latter, I recall the solemnly dramatic burial of Pius IX. in St. Peter's, which I had the privilege of witnessing. It was at night, and the vast edifice was in darkness save for the constellation of lamps that always burn around the tomb of the apostle, a few great candles that stood here and there on pedestals, and those borne by the mournful procession. Their gleams fell fitfully on white monuments in the indefinite recesses of aisles and chapels, and cast Rembrandt-like shadows and lights on sculptured hierarchs and apostles. The uncoffined body of the dead high-priest, robed in scarlet and crowned with the tiara, was borne

down the central nave and around the balda-
chin of St. Peter to the chapel of the choir, followed by the helmeted "Noble Guard," ermined
cardinals, empurpled monsignori, and a few
favored spectators in deep black. In the foreground, majestic in form and attitude, stood St.
Mark upon his pedestal, with outstretched hand
pointing to the mural recess far above the tessel-
lated pavement, and revealed by a solitary taper
inside, where a departed pope sleeps until his
successor claims his place. At every one of these
rites, for centuries past, the inexorable hand of the
marble apostle relegates to rest the marble pontiff.

No such startling realism can be offered by the
flatness of paint and sheen of gilding in the Greek
Church. But, on the other hand, the music of the
latter is far grander and more artistic than that of
the Roman Church ; and the habiliments of the
priests, the details of the service, and the devoutness of the people make an effect superior in

grace, dignity, and impressiveness. It would require a volume to describe the relics and sacerdo-
tal ornaments which we saw in the Church of the
Assumption and others within the Kremlin.
Prominent among them was a book of gospels
presented by the mother of Peter the Great, in
binding of solid gold studded with precious
stones, valued at £50,000 ; it weighs one hundred pounds, and requires two men to lift it.
We were carried back to the days of the Emperor
Constantine when we looked at the great gold
cross incrusted with emeralds, rubies, etc., which
belonged to him, and pageants of all earthly
pomp were figured in the coronation-crowns and
gorgeous vestments of patriarchs and bishops.
The latter are principally in the sacristy of the
Holy Synod ; chief among them is a crimson-
velvet robe worn by the patriarchs of Moscow
when they were consecrated, thickly embroidered
with pearls and precious stones, and plates of

gold with sacred devices in *niello* work are interspersed, making the entire weight of the vestment
fifty-four pounds.   Ivan the Terrible, one of the
worst of the early Tsars, presented it in expiation
of the murder of his own son !

Very many of the sacred vestments and vessels
are expiatory offerings of sovereigns, or gifts to
prove their piety.   Some of the robes are covered
with pictorial representations of the whole sacred
drama, from the Annunciation to the Ascen-
sion.

The mitres are like domes surmounted by ornate crosses ; one of them has a ground of blue
damask, bordered with ermine ; the Saviour, the
Virgin, and numerous saints, in gold, pearls, and
stones, decorate the surface, and inscriptions in
pearls fill the intervening spaces.   Two of them run
thus :   "Look down upon us from Thy heavens, O
Lord !"   "I put all my confidence in thee, Mother
of God ; take me under thy holy protection."

All the precious stones added to this mitre give it the weight of five and a half pounds.

I pass by the beautiful crosses of every sort—the pectorals, the altar-crosses, and those carried in processions with banners of such bulk and wondrous color and design as never are seen out of Russia; but I pause a moment at the glass cases within which are the rare and lovely *panagias*, or pectoral images worn by bishops. Some of them are of enamelled gold ornamented with rubies and pearls, and cameo figures of saints in the centre; another is a sardonyx nearly four inches long, cut in three strata,—on the upper one being the Virgin and Child, in Byzantine design; a third is a superb ruby engraved with the Annunciation, set in gold and diamonds; and the fourth, a jasper encircled with colored jewels, presents a bas-relief of the Madonna among clouds, with arms upraised in prayer.

Before leaving the churches of the Kremlin,

the marvel and the beauty of which I have but
touched with the tip of a flying wing, I return for
a moment to the Cathedral of the Assumption,
where I must mention a miracle-working Virgin,
attributed to St. Luke. It found its way hither
from Kief in the twelfth century, is believed to
have forced the flight of Tamerlane from Russia,
and its jewels, estimated at £45,000 (one emerald
alone being worth £10,000), gleam in the twilight of the edifice with an almost supernatural
light.

At the approach of the French army all the
most precious articles from the churches were
secreted by the priests ; but nevertheless the soldiers carried off from this one alone five tons of
silver and five hundred pounds in gold. Oblong
tombs of patriarchs and bishops stand around the
walls ; those most highly venerated are in the four
corners, the place of honor here as in the Orient ;
without effigy or sculpture, these sarcophagi re-

CATHEDRAL OF ST. MICHAEL THE ARCHANGEL—IN THE
KREMLIN.

semble, as Gautier said, "great trunks made for the journey of eternity."

Turning from the splendor of these "lamps of sacrifice," we drove to the spacious Foundling Hospital, which stands in its own pretty park. We sent our cards to the Superior, who received us courteously, and conversed in fluent French while she escorted us through the well-ordered establishment. The rooms are all of great size, clean and airy, but very simply and scantily furnished. In the first one a number of neatly-dressed children, from five to ten years old, were at dinner. They rose and saluted us like little ladies and gentlemen as they were—orphans, we were told, of good birth and property, but without relatives, and therefore sent here until old enough for school-education.

We then walked through five or six long rooms, in each of which there were at least sixty babies —the "foundlings," proper. Only two of them could be called pretty ; and their unattractiveness of type was emphasized by the look of weary im-becility and old age that many new-born infants wear. Sixteen thousand are received every year ; about a third are illegitimate, and the remainder are brought by parents too poor to take care of them.

Their tiny cribs were ranged in two long rows down the centre of the rooms ; and in front of them stood two rows of nurses, wearing short white sleeves, many strings of beads on their bare necks, and high white caps from which hung streamers of red or blue ribbons. Russian nurses wear blue when the baby in charge is a boy, and red when it is a girl. These peasant-women were in *grande tenue* that day, as it was Sunday, when vis-itors are expected (the every-day dress is doubtless less coquettish), but their irregular Calmuck feat-ures were stolid and unresponsive. Those who had not babies at their breasts bowed very low, according to the fashion of the country, as we approached. The Matron was anxious to exhibit every part of the institution, and we could not with politeness decline; and thus we were shown the chapel, where the infants are baptized immediately on arrival, if that rite has not been previously performed; the book in which their numbers and names are recorded, when a corresponding label is tied around the infant neck; baths of copper lined with thick flannel; presses full of coarse but soft linen, and down-pillows on which they are dressed. Excellent physicians are provided, and every comfort for the little waifs during the four weeks of their stay; after that they are sent, together with their nurses, to the villages where the latter belong. About two rubles a month (from a dollar to a dollar and a half) are allowed for their maintenance, but more than half of them die from the rigor of the·climate and unsuitable food.

With all reverence for the gentle humanity of

this hospital, the sight of these helpless, homeless little beings was most pitiful. The four weeks within those sheltering walls are doubtless to very many the least wretched of their lives.

### RUSSIAN MONASTIC INSTITUTIONS.

Monasteries and convents are much alike everywhere since they have ceased to be receptacles of learning or refuges from outside barbarism ; but in order to compare those in Russia with others in Western Europe, we visited two of the oldest and most revered. The Devichi Convent in Moscow has been for three hundred and fifty years a sanctuary for Tsarinas and other high-born ladies, many of whom are buried within its fortressed walls. Passing through a grand gateway, we entered a cemetery of tombs more or less pretentious, inclosed in gilded iron railings, and guarded by crosses and images of saints. Intermingled are several churches in the usual ornate style, the dwellings of the nuns, and simpler graves in every available spot, abundant flowers on the surface, but the "conqueror worm" beneath, revelling in his own domain. It was the hour for morning Mass in the principal chapel, and we obtained places near the choir, which was composed entirely of nuns. Their voices had neither sweetness nor power, and they were very unattractive women, sallow, dark, and of ascetic pallor. Perhaps their hideous veils were partly responsible ; few faces could stand the test of thick black serge, standing high and rigid on the head like an iron crown, and falling in long folds over a dress of the same funereal character.

An abbess received us in her simple parlor with much courtesy, and led us the usual round of the pharmacy, the hospital, and the refectory. The nuns whom we saw without veils had pleasant faces ; the wooden floors were clean, tables and beds covered with white linen, pictured saints and burning lamps in every room, but no evidence of occupation except in the work-room, where were many specimens of embroidery on muslin, not original and rather expensive. In the dark crypt-like refectory were long, narrow tables set with the conventual coarse linen and iron spoons, and with bread of dark unsifted wheat, not unpalatable and doubtless more wholesome than the fine quality now disapproved by medical science.

The abbess proudly led us through a cavernous brick passage to the kitchen, which was in fine order for exhibition that day, as it offered the unusual luxury of a meat-soup and an insipid pink jelly, in honor of the fête-day of the Superior.

We asked whether the nuns visit the sick or instruct children ; and the reply was, " No : they say their prayers and embroider." Thus the pallid lives of these well-born ladies are not even brightened by the gracious tints of charity and good works.

Among other gentle amenities of the French invasion was the attempt to destroy this convent by putting barrels of gunpowder in the crypt of the principal church and igniting a stream of spirits which they directed towards it. Several courageous nuns succeeded in extinguishing the flames.

We started at eight o'clock one morning to take the train for Troitsa, in order to pass a few hours at the celebrated monastery of St. Sergius. It was always a pleasure, except for the atrocious pavements, to drive through the streets of this fascinating city. Moujiks alone were astir, more in harmony with the scene than their conventional masters. No women were visible, and in truth the old Asiatic habit of seclusion still retains a certain influence. We passed the large white station of the Siberia railway, and shuddered at thought of the agonized exiles to whom it has been a portal of despair.

*Lasciate ogni speranza, voi ch' entrate qui.*

From another station our train took us northward forty miles through a pretty undulating
country marked by villages, gardens, and green-
domed churches. The first appearance of the
" holy, ancient, and monastic pile " is very striking ; on a slightly elevated hill a quadrilateral,
with very high white walls twenty feet thick, and
eight fortified towers, incloses an imposing group
of domed churches resplendent with the usual
decorations. It was built more than five hundred years ago by St. Sergius—a man so eminent
for piety that potentates came from afar to seek his
blessing, and native sovereigns in return enriched
the monastery with large grants of land. In the
last century it owned a hundred thousand serfs, and
the treasures within are unaccountable. It with-
stood several sieges of Tartars and Poles, was a
refuge for innumerable pilgrims, as well as for
Peter the Great during the insurrection of the
Streltzi, and fortunately the French never found

their way here—all which exemptions are attributed
to the miracle-working portrait of St. Sergius.
Within the walls is a miniature city, more brilliantly
Oriental than the Orient itself : ten churches, the
palaces of the Tsar and the Archimandrite, the
refectory, cells of the monks, and treasure-rooms
are planted without regularity, at any convenient
point.  There are no cloisters, but no hue of the
rainbow is lacking : bright blue, red, pale green,
and profuse gold inside, and outside, under the
blue of the sky, the gold of the sun and the
opaque white of the walls make a dizzy riot of
color which, here as in Moscow, when gently
toned by time is continually renewed.

Service was proceeding in the Church of the
Trinity, and we made our way, through the most
picturesque and evil-smelling crowd we had yet
encountered, to the most weird of all interiors.
The same long rows of unearthly figures on gold
backgrounds stretch in perspective down the

walls, stand on pillars, or start like phantoms
from angles, revealed by a sudden light and
shrinking back as it retires. The Ikonostas,
which rises to the vaulted ceiling, is incomparably
rich in precious stones around the aureoles of
sainted hierarchs ; in close proximity is the silver-
gilt tomb of St. Sergius, glittering with lamps and
a canopy supported by four columns all of the
same metal : around it knelt a group of pilgrims
with long white beards and some noble faces
illumined with faith and fervor ; desolate beggars
in brown rags with yellow lights, their legs bound
in rags strapped on like a classic cothurnus ;
moujiks in dull reds and blues, prostrating, sign-
ing the cross, kissing the sacred tomb ; while
above them scintillated the prismatic hues of
rubies, sapphires, and diamonds, irradiating here
and there an uplifted head or a suppliant hand
—a most typical picture which nothing in Western Europe can repeat. We visited the rooms

where monks were copying with patient fidelity
pictures of saints in colored draperies and golden
glories, the shop where they are sold, and the
treasuries of priestly paraphernalia presented by
high personages, and not inferior to those in the
Kremlin.   Again are vestments embroidered with
pearls and precious stones, forming flowers, figures,
and Sclavonic inscriptions ; Bibles and liturgies enamelled in arabesque patterns overlaid with rubies,
emeralds, and sapphires of great size and splendor ;
sacred vessels of gold with rims of diamonds ;
strings of pearls, and crowns, crosses, caskets,
vases, chandeliers : a Nile-like overflow of riches,
each object the expression of a spiritual sentiment
—of gratitude, of faith, or of remorse.

But we could not linger in these rooms ; the
windows seemed to have been sealed for centuries,
and to the asphyxiating atmosphere was added the
intolerable odor from an unwashed crowd.   It is
said that cholera and plague have never entered

these holy walls ; and if that is true, Science may as well burn its books on cleanliness and ventilation. The fraternity live the same self-centred lives as the nuns of the convent Devichi ; painting takes the place of embroidery—*voilà tout!*

A few miles distant are some old catacombs inhabited by men who have vowed seclusion from the light of day and the face of man ; needless to say, we did not disturb their enjoyment.

### IN GENERAL.

There seems no end to the sights of Moscow : museums, private picture-galleries, drives to parks, and excursions outside, as well as theatres where, even when ignorant of the language, the costumes and manners of the country will entertain.

The Gostinnoi Dvor, or Bazaar, is a labyrinth of shops as small as those on the Ponte Vecchio in Florence, filled with cheap wares from all the provinces of the empire ; in the silversmiths' row are pretty trifles for souvenirs, for which, however, one must bargain or pay extortionately.

Very near the Bazaar is the most extraordinary church in Moscow ; nor does another like it exist in any part of the world. At evening it seems a fantastic mirage or the architecture of cloud-land painted by sunset. It is a sort of Hindoo pagoda, containing nine chapels linked together internally by a maze of narrow corridors ; it has no centre, and each part is different from and independent of all the others. One cupola is carved like an artichoke, another like a pineapple, a third resembles a melon, a fourth a Turkish turban, and five more are of various designs,—all colored, as well as the body of the edifice, with the entire chromatic scale, enhanced by silver and gold. This wild creation, which is called the Church of St. Basil, the patron saint of idiots, or the *Vasili Blajennoi*, was another of the expiatory offerings of John the Terrible for the murder of his son—

CHURCH OF ST. BASIL—MOSCOW.

much on the principle of the monumental effigies
with folded hands

" Who seek for life-long evil to atone
By ceaseless orisons in stone."

The climax of all the dazzling and half-barbaric
opulence of historic and hereditary souvenirs is
found in the Imperial Treasury.   From the palace
of the Tsars an immense staircase closed by a trellised iron gate leads to this receptacle of gifts
from sultans and shahs, tributes of alliance with
wild Asiatic chiefs, tokens of commercial traffic,
—in short, the assembled Lares and Penates of all
centuries past.

We enter first the Armory, where four sentinels
in old Sclavonic armor, mounted on strangely-
caparisoned horses, never leave their posts, but
guard with perpetual vigilance the trophies, flags,
standards, and fire-arms which are grouped on
walls and around pillars that support the vaulted

roof. I have seen the finest armories in Europe; but none equals the interest of this, because it bears the stamp of a different civilization. The art is lost of making the damascened blades and helmets accumulated here ; the banners are most pictorial and superb : one of the sixteenth century exhibits on a star-spangled field an image of Christ with a host of saints and seraphim on horseback (!) and a cloud of heavenly witnesses in the background. There are coats of mail engraved with texts from the Koran ; scimitars and daggers with handles incrusted with turquoises and precious stones.

In another room we salute the entire Romanoff family, with whose positive features and tall, muscular forms we have now become familiar. Peter the Great was our favorite ; his bluff, swarthy face, keen black eyes, and resolute mouth show the indomitable will, overflow of brain, and rough self-assertion that rank him as Ursus Major in the

planisphere of sovereigns. Every object that illustrates his life is interesting, from his big boots to
the miniature carriage with mica windows in
which as a child he was driven around the
paternal park ; and we admire for his sake, even
more than all the other resplendent crowns in
this treasury, the one he had made for his peasant-
wife, which contains 2536 diamonds, besides a
ruby of almost inestimable value.

The room of royal insignia contains an op-
pressive mass of gold, precious stones, and gorgeous apparel. There are the Kazan and Astra-
khan crowns before they were united with Russia,
and that of Vladimir Monomaque, whose wife
was the daughter of Harold, king of England, at
the time of the battle of Hastings—compounds of
pearls and jewels counted by the hundreds, and
held together by filigree gold with Greek crosses
at the top.

The sceptre of Vladimir, about a yard in length,

contains 270 large diamonds and 300 rubies and emeralds. Another crown possesses 900 diamonds, and the cross rises from an immense ruby. Among the regalia now used at coronations is a girdle of large diamonds ; a sceptre containing the great diamond Lazaref, one of the largest known ; the emperor's crown, made entirely of diamonds, a row of immense pearls, and an uncut ruby an inch long. The empress's crown is equally rich, but smaller, and is fastened on with diamond hair-pins. A curious relic is the chain of Michael, the first of the Romanoffs, composed of ninety-nine rings, each of which is engraved with one of his titles, accompanied by a short prayer.

The beauty of workmanship in all these baubles is as remarkable as their value.

The velvet state robes are as ornate as those in the sacristy of the Synod, and thrones of ancient date might verify the biblical stories of " King Solomon in all his glory." One that came from

Persia is of ivory studded with 875 diamonds, 1223 rubies, besides turquoises and pearls innumerable. One great room is devoted to many hundred articles of all ages and countries, for state use and decoration, in the way of pitchers, goblets, vases, candelabra, etc., of gold and silver with every wild variation of ornamentation, high and low relief.

In view of the accumulated wealth in churches, palaces, monasteries, and treasuries throughout the empire, Monte Cristo's caves and Scheherezade's fables appear very credible possibilities ; and though tolerably familiar with similar collections in other countries, we said a few days later, as we sauntered through the Green Vaults at Dresden, "There is nothing really splendid outside of Russia." However, everything has its point of advantage ; we were sated with splendor ; we declared we never wanted to see another diamond ; and swinging the pendulum to the extreme tip of its arc, we exclaimed, "Give us love in a hut, with water and a crust !"

No one can study Moscow for even a few days without feeling an interest and admiration that few cities can inspire. Others are palimpsests of change and perhaps progression ; Moscow resists new inscriptions and clings to its sacred past. We were more than ever sympathetic with it when we looked down from the "Sparrows' Hill," four miles distant, on the broad panorama of its stately architecture with its golden fringe of minarets and domes. This was the view which first met the eyes of Napoleon when he stood on this hill, seventy-four years ago, and watched the advance of his eager battalions from three different points. But no Russian forces appeared to contest the way, and an ominous stillness pervaded the air. The emperor galloped with his staff to one of the barriers and halted there, expecting to receive the keys of the city. He might as well have waited for her-

alds from a city of the dead : three hundred thousand inhabitants were flying northward, and only
sufferers in hospitals and prisoners in dungeons
remained to mock the entrance of "*la grande
armée.*" Then began the holocaust previously
prepared by the Muscovites of their beloved and
revered city ; the conflagration lasted three days,
and the mortified invader found himself the mark
of the scorn and reproach of all Europe. The
familiar details of the tragedy are recalled by the
traveller with painful realism.

We returned to St. Petersburg for a day, and
then took the rail for Berlin. As far as the German
frontier at Eydkuhnen, twenty-four hours, the carriages, the stations, and rail afford entire comfort, though the scenery has no interest ; the remaining twelve hours the railway is very rough.

Our Russian Days had ceased to be, and our
Norway Nights were poems of the past. Sun,

moon, and stars resumed possession of the sky ;
we had come back to the tyranny of dates and
divisions of time ; the Hour to Retire walked in
with his lamp, the Hour to Rise threw open the
window.   No longer, for the year of grace 1886,
could be found the gladsome inconsequence of
*" l'heure qui plait à votre Majesté."*